Complete Horoscope 2020

Monthly astrological forecasts for every Zodiac sign for 2020

TATIANA BORSCH

CONTENTS

General Annual Forecast
For Every Sign

ARIES

The most important thing for the coming year is to stay ahead of the game; there should be no holding back. Problems are there to be solved and, as far as Aries is concerned, the only way is to face up to a challenge!

Business. The first six months of the year, from January to June, is the best time for all professional and financial projects. During this period, entrepreneurs will strengthen their positions, expand their influence and make lucrative deals.

Clerical workers will have a great chance to climb the promotion ladder. For some this will happen within their company, while others will prosper by moving to a new company. In this respect January, April and the first half of May are especially promising.

During the first half of the year, co-operation with colleagues from other cities or overseas will not cause any problems. But as from the second half of May, the situation will change as a result of emerging tensions and friction in working relationships. At first, this may not appear serious, but the situation will gradually worsen and lead to difficulties.
The second half of the year is a difficult period both for clerical workers and businessmen.
It's possible that entrepreneurs will fall foul of their business partners or those in power. The confrontation might be of a serious nature but is like-

ly to have ended by December. There is a good chance of overall success, but it will be necessary to do the hard miles first.

Clerical workers are likely to have conflict with management in the second half of the year. This may well be down to you. You might allow previous success to go to your head and so become arrogant and perhaps a little ill-disciplined; this leads to mutual resentment and is possibly followed by dismissal.

In a different scenario, this period will be marked by the beginning of changes in company fortunes. You might become overly anxious and lose self-confidence. The situation will settle down by December and you will realise that any recent difficulties have, in fact, opened doors for you.

Money. You needn't worry about money in the first half of the year as income will be regular and it will grow. The second half of the year is more difficult. Although it is unlikely that you will face economic ruin, some uncertainty and concerns for the future are possible. This situation is a little like a game of roulette – be careful when deciding on the red or the black!

Love and family. In your personal life, it is likely that you'll face changes in the second half of the year. There are no changes in family and romantic relationships in the period from January to June; everything will remain as it was. However, in the second half of the year, Mars moves into Aries and stays there for seven months instead of the usual seven weeks. This suggests major changes in your personal life. Any harboured discontentment or grievances might be aired suddenly and unexpectedly. In the most difficult cases it might even mean an end to the relationship or divorce. If spouses work together or are too tied up with work, the situation will be worse. Even though it might be unbearably hard at times, you would be well advised to keep your head down, hold your tongue and wait for things to blow over.
Your relationship with close family members will worsen significantly. It will start in June and get worse.

Health. Your energy levels are sufficiently high in 2020 and you shouldn't have to worry about your health, although emotional strains in the second half of the year might knock you out of your stride. In this case, keep self-discipline and faith that any misfortunes will pass.

TAURUS

2020 will be a bit of an obstacle course. Unfortunately, dreams are not always handed to you on a silver platter. You should remember this and try to stay in the saddle. Anyway, you have very little choice!

Business. The coming year could be described as a game of two halves. The first half of the year, from January to June, is quite a stable and predictable time.

Entrepreneurs and officials of various levels will co-operate well with colleagues from other cities or overseas and will work hard to achieve their goals. You might even plan to move or to launch a new business far from your home. At the beginning of 2020, the situation might seem stable and predictable.

However, it will all change in the second half of the year. You will have to deal with red tape and various other problems. Each case will be different; sometimes serious legal issues that jeopardise recent achievements, sometimes the unprofessional and even hostile attitude of your partners from other cities or overseas.

Those who do not plan co-operation with overseas partners should prepare for unexpected and exhausting inspections that will test your limits in the second half of the year to December.
Clerical workers are likely to face difficulties from other staff in the office; these range from underground rumours and gossip to open conflict. You cannot change this, so prepare yourself and do not be caught on the back foot. If you are to withstand the onslaught of the planets, hold fast and believe in yourself. The situation will improve at the end of December or in January-February 2021.

This is good news to all active professionals of your sign.

Money. The financial forecast for 2020 is quite mixed.
In the first half of the year, business develops predictably and even if you don't make a good profit, neither will you suffer any serious financial losses. According to the astrologer, the second half of the year will be unsta-

ble and volatile for not only financial but for legal and ethical reasons and your finances will be affected.

Love and family. 2020 could be considered as a crossroads not only in work, but also in your personal life. This is because the planet of change - Uranus - has been nicely settled in your birth sign for a long time. With the help of Uranus, you will change like a snake shedding its skin. Is that a good thing? Definitely! But reaching the next level demands hard work, and this will be your task in 2020.

You will face dramatic changes in your family relationships. In the second half of the year, problems with close family members are possible. It may be either a serious falling out or other major family issues. The situation will be resolved by December, but only with joint efforts. Until then, you need to keep a sense of perspective and try to solve any problems gradually, one step at a time.

In 2020, some people will plan to move to a different city or even abroad. In the first half of the year everything may go according to plan, although in the second half of the year you will have to overcome various unexpected difficulties. There might be legal problems or other situations which are out of your control and seem quite impossible. However, time will pass, the planets will calm, and everything will fall into place; but not earlier than December.

Health. Your energy levels are quite high this year, but the stars strongly suggest being extra careful while travelling and driving as the second half of 2020 does not look so good in this respect.

GEMINI

2020 is a transition period for you - if you feel like just dropping everything and starting again, this is exactly what you should do.

Business. When it comes to business, this year could hardly be considered favourable. Many ideas you have been developing will now seem boring and pointless. It is time to forget them and to think of something new, something more challenging and interesting.

Entrepreneurs and higher management might consider selling their business - or a part of it - and launching a new enterprise. The end of 2019 and the first half of 2020 are a good time for this. Those who run a construction business or work with land and property will be highly successful. It is also a good time for capital purchases, and these will be a good foundation for lucrative future deals.

Clerical workers will consider changing jobs, but this will only be possible at the end of 2020 at the earliest. It is worth thinking everything over carefully and not rushing into anything.

The second half of the year is a stressful and dramatic period. It's possible that there will be serious conflict with friends, close associates or senior officials. The reasons might be money, valuable property or mutual obligations. The situation is not stable, but it will be sorted out in either December 2020 or February 2021.

Closer to the end of the year, many Gemini will think about moving to a different place - in many cases this will be a place you have visited many times before. Some will make this decisive move in December, others in 2021.

Money. Financially, the first half of 2020 is quite prosperous. You might profit from real estate business or bank deposits. It is also possible that you may be able to get a loan on seemingly favourable terms.

Those who are not involved in business can rely on the support of parents or partners. In the second half of the year, you will likely be in the red as many of your birth sign will have to pay back outstanding debts, make loan repayments and cover old financial liabilities. So, when dealing with your finances in the more favourable first half of the year, don't forget about the challenging second half of the year to come - try to eliminate risks and losses.

Love and family. Your personal life is driven by past events. Many of your sign will think about purchasing new accommodation and this can be done at various times throughout 2020. In this case, there will be significant expenditure in the period from July to December; this is, of course, a natural consequence of buying a new property.

This year is challenging both for romantic relationships and for unsettled families. In the second half of the year things might go wrong; you might be involved in a spate of accusations and conflicts and only some will be able to withstand this.

Some Gemini will consider the possibility of moving house. You might also move to a new country - somewhere you have already lived or visited many times before.

Health. Your energy levels are not high in 2020and so you should take good care of yourself and keep everything within normal limits.

CANCER

Bringing back something or someone from your past will not lead anywhere. In the first half of the year everything seems rosy enough, but in the second half of the year you finally see cold, hard reality. This is true both in working and romantic relationships.

Business. 2020 might be controversial professionally. The beginning of the year is quite favourable and there may be co-operation with people you already know. They might be your former partners, some old friends or even an old flame and everything will go smoothly at the beginning.

However, the second half of the year will be more difficult and demanding. It will turn out that your colleagues have a different vision regarding the development of the business and its future. It is also possible that you will have differing opinions about investments and the contribution of each participant. Misunderstandings, arguments and possible distribution of joint assets may result. You should also understand that your position looks weak and it might be you who has to back down.
In a different scenario, you might have problems with authorities who put obstacles in front of you.

Some changes will take place for clerical workers, and these might turn out to be quite painful. As a result, many of your sign may need to think about other ways to apply their talents. The most difficult period in this respect will be from June to December.

Co-operation with colleagues from other cities or overseas is not stable; some projects are successful while others are not. This requires your constant attention and control.

Those who have legal problems might find themselves in a serious situation, especially when your lawyers are either slow or incompetent or both.

Money. This is a heck of a year financially. The financial situation is up and down. Closer to December you will have to admit that you actually are in the red. If you are lucky, you will break even.

Love and family. For many Cancerians, the main battles of 2020 will take place within the family. It is especially serious for those couples who have already had some troubles. It is not unlikely that an old love will come back into circulation or that your ex-spouse might want reconciliation; you might even decide to give your relationship with them another chance. At the beginning of the year all is smooth, but in the second half of the year it will become clear that you have again been caught in the same old trap. It is hard to understand who is to blame, but that doesn't really matter; the main thing is that it did not work out.

If spouses are co-owners of business or property, it will make the situation even more complicated. Beware! It is possible that in the case of a break-up you will be left with nothing as your now ex-partner is determined and will not budge an inch regarding money.
Strong couples, with the help of their love and wisdom, will be able to overcome all obstacles together.

Health. Your energy levels are not good in 2020 and you might regularly suffer from apathy and fatigue. This will be more evident in the second half of the year which will turn out to be a considerably difficult period.

LEO

You are fully committed for the whole year. You will make the progress you have been striving for, but don't forget to cover your back!

Business. Let's start with good news. In the first half of the year, you will progress and grow professionally. Entrepreneurs will continue to develop a business launched in the autumn of 2019. By May, you will have achieved something quite remarkable and made quite a profit.

Clerical workers can expect significant career opportunities. For some it will be promotion within the current company, for others it means a new job with good prospects.

However, the bad news is that in the second half of the year a seemingly stable situation will start to change. It might be because of inspections or old legal problems or it might be because of the hostile attitude of business partners from other cities and overseas. This will influence not only the business relationship but will take a heavy toll on all deals. You should remember this in the first half of the year, when the situation is more favourable, especially if you work with distant partners. The problems will be serious and are likely to linger until December.

Clerical workers will find their employers subject to a very thorough inspection or audit that will undoubtedly affect the business and employment climate.

The stars warn Leos about possible problems in the second half of the year. This is no time to let your guard down and you should be cautious in the middle of summer, especially in July.

Money. In the first half of 2020 - in January, in the second half of April and the first half of May - your income will become remarkably stable. In the second half of the year, September looks quite promising.

Love and family. For romantic relationships, 2020 does not look at all good - probably because your work and numerous other responsibilities consume all your time. Only at the end of the year, in the second half of

December, will single people meet somebody interesting with the possibility of a happy future together. If you are an incurable workaholic, you might begin an exciting office affair in the first half of the year.

During the second half of the year, many families will have some troubles with relatives. For some it means an argument, for others it means problems with close relatives.

It is possible that you will have to sit at a relative's bedside for quite a long period. The stars advise you to consider all outcomes with care and prepare for possible problems in advance so as not to be caught unawares.

Health. In 2020, for various reasons, many born under your sign will start a new and healthy way of life. This year will be a good time to do sport, to stick to a healthy diet and to focus on regular self-care.
Be more careful while travelling and driving in the second half of the year.

VIRGO

The coming year will be a period of creativity, change and conflict. In a way, it reminds us of a fairy tale with the gentle beginning, the hero or heroine facing the challenge in the middle and then the traditional happy ending.

Business. For professionally active Virgos, the period from January to June will be favourable. This is a good time both for promoting your projects and for finding new and useful contacts. It is also a good time to renew relationships with colleagues and partners.

This is an excellent time for people in the creative professions; demand for their work will grow and lead to increased income. The stars recommend considering all aspects of any future co-operation carefully, and to study all documents closely - especially financial ones. It is possible that in the second half of the year, you face some unexpected or unpredictable circumstances that will be detrimental to business and to co-operation.
Most problems will happen at the end of June, July, August and October. If you are sensible, however, all difficult situations will be resolved by the end of December or the beginning of 2021.

Clerical workers should be more accurate when carrying out their responsibilities because there will be situations when they need to stay calm and to prove their professionalism. You will be tested almost to your limits - remember this and stay ahead of the pack.

Money. Financially, the first half of the year is quiet, and everything goes according to plan. However, in the second half of the year you will have to confront a financial crisis at its worst. Those who deal with finances and material issues should be especially cautious. There is a strong possibility of financial losses or unexpected expenses; you should try to anticipate them and not take risks!

Those who do not run a business will need to solve family problems connected with children and this will take the lion's share of your family finances.

Love and family. The coming year will bring serious changes to your personal life. The first half of the year will bring old friends and lovers back to you. The period from June to December is a time when you must re-examine and evaluate the true value of your relationships and consider just what it is that you expect from your life. At the end of the year you will need to make a final decision and it is more than likely that there will be some sort of break-up. This forecast is mainly true for lovers, but also for unsteady friendships and unhappy romantic relationships.

Strong couples will again become concerned about their children's future and will invest a large part of their family budget in their education and training. It is also possible that your children will have some problems that require extra expenditure.

All unpleasant situations will happen during the second, quite stressful part of 2020.

In many families, 2020 will be marked with the birth of children and/or grandchildren. If the addition to your family is expected in the second half of the year, you should pay extra attention to the pregnancy and choose only experienced maternity staff for the delivery.

Health. In the first half of the year you are in good health and full of energy; you will be free of any sickness. The second, less favourable, part of the year will bring some stressful situations, and there is the possibility of injury. You should avoid any risky situations and be mindful of excess.

LIBRA

In 2020 you will face seemingly impossible situations. Your task is simply not to lose - you will prevail!

Business. In the first half of the year, entrepreneurs and top managers will consider expanding their business and for this reason, they will purchase larger premises or more land.
This will go smoothly at first, without any obstacles and red tape. However, closer to the middle of the year, the situation will change. Your rivals, either domestic or from overseas and those with whom you have had prior confrontation, will try to bleed you dry.

As from the beginning of June, the situation becomes threatening. In July, your opponents will start to actually act against you and this will be much tougher than you could ever have imagined.

The second half of the year will be really stressful. It is a good idea to be ready to defend yourself and to find some allies. Unfortunately, there will not be many allies, and so you will have to mostly rely on yourself. You should be cautious of your assistants and employees as not all of them are trustworthy, reliable or competent. You need to put together your own team to face the difficult times ahead.

The situation for clerical workers is not stable due to possible changes in management and company structure. As a wise Chinese man - Confucius – once said, 'God save us from living in changing times'. You should stay in the shadows and not bombard your management with requests; you may be misunderstood.

A run of bad luck will come to an end by the end of December and it is likely that you will get what you deserve. In 2021, people will comment that, 'Winners are not judged!'.

Money. Financially, the first half of the year looks good. During this period, you can count on not only your own wages, but also on lucrative property deals, an inheritance or favourable loan conditions. Some Librans may expect support from parents or family members.

The second half of the year is less stable, with possible problems in business or in personal relationships.

Love and family. Those whose focus is personal relationships, might experience hard times. In this respect, the second half of the year does not look good. Couples experiencing tension in their relationship might begin the process of separation. Mutual property such as apartments, houses or country houses will become the bones of contention. You might also have problems with a long-divorced partner. Your spouse's position will turn out to be rigid, unyielding and aggressive. You should be able to grind out a compromise that suits both sides, but only by the end of December. It might well be that your children will act as peace makers.

In some cases, we cannot talk about a final reconciliation but only about resolving a painful property issue.

Strong couples might purchase a house, a flat, a country house or invest in the family business. They will spend the second half of the year fighting claims on property they legally own.

The first half of the year is quite a predictable time when Librans will consider some serious changes in their day to day lives. Gradually and steadily, they will resolve many situations by July. You should be cautious when signing purchase contracts. Also, do not forget that the second half of the year will be a stressful period.

Relationships with your children are valuable, and they will likely need more of your attention, care and money.

It is quite difficult to give a forecast to those who are in romantic relationship, but many will decide to start living together and will overcome any possible difficulties in the second part of the year. If you have not been so lucky in love, don't despair! The world is a big place and your soulmate is out there somewhere!

Health. Your energy levels are not high in 2020, so don't test your body and stick to your limits. Many of your birth sign might start gaining weight, so don't forget about doing exercise, taking walks in the country-side and keeping to a balanced diet.

SCORPIO

In 2020, it will become clear that one stage in your life has come to an end and that a completely new story awaits you. So, prepare for some changes!

Business. In 2020, many Scorpions will be interested in co-operation with colleagues from other cities and overseas and will strive towards a long-cherished goal. There is the possibility of moving to a different place, of starting a business in a different city or overseas but there will be worries and problems connected with this. In the first half of the year, everything is predictable, and you will achieve a lot. New partners appear on the horizon, and relationships with some of your old colleagues will be revitalized.

Many of your birth sign will join the business of older relatives and everything progresses well at the outset. But as from June, however, the situation will start to change for the worse; some problems from the past will resurface.

Moving to a new place and running business there might mean a legal challenge. In other cases, you might also face some legal problems, or the return of some old problems.

Entrepreneurs and top managers should prepare for inspections, possibly challenging ones, in June. Looking further forward, all situations starting in the second half of the year have negative after-effects that will not finish before December. 2021, however, will be more benevolent.

Clerical workers will have some disagreements with their colleagues in the second half of 2020. There are possible changes to the structure of their companies that lead to stress and anxiety. As a result, you might start looking for a new job or start your own business in 2021.

Money. Financially, the first half of the year is more or less neutral. You can expect neither large gains nor serious losses. The situation may be much worse in the second half of the year and this is a natural consequence of the issues you face - you need to steel yourself against any coming problems.

Love and family. Changes are also possible in your personal life. Many of you will decide to change where you live, and you will take the first steps towards this at the beginning of the year. In some cases, the move might be to do with your relatives and they will help you to settle in the new place.

Some Scorpions will renew a relationship with an old flame who lives in a different city or overseas and moving there may be the natural outcome of your story.

Many of your sign will go to study in a different city or abroad and at the beginning everything seems fine. However, from the beginning of June/July, something will go wrong and almost all Scorpions will face a series of problems.

These might include unexpected problems with relatives, the laws in a different country or difficulties in studying. You should remember this and try to soften any blows but if you cannot prevent such situations, take one step at a time and remember that, 'a journey of a thousand miles begins with a single step'.

Health. Your energy levels are high in 2020; you are strong, healthy, dynamic and adventurous and will attract a lot of attention. You can expect to make some new acquaintances and those who are single might even meet their soulmate.

In the second half of the year, you should be extra careful on trips and when driving – the possibility of accidents, injuries and unpleasant incidents is quite high.

SAGITTARIUS

You will be swept off your feet by the run of events in 2020 and it will be difficult to handle. Even if you do get swept away, try to keep a tight grip on both your feelings and finances.

Business. In the first half of the year, most professionals of your birth sign will have a good chance to climb the promotion ladder and significantly improve their credentials. It might be not exactly what you have dreamt of, but in the course of time, you will come to value the importance of these changes and prospects.

There will be increased finances and good prospects for future. Entrepreneurs can expect lucrative deals; clerical workers can expect promotion with a substantial wage increase.

In the second half of the year, the situation will take a turn for the worse. Entrepreneurs will need to invest in numerous projects - many more than expected. The period from July to December may turn out to be ruinous; all your hard-won earnings may disappear.

Closer to the end of the year, many Sagittarians will develop a plan to move to a new place or start a business in a different city or abroad. The realization of these plans will take place in 2021.

Money. Financially, 2020 will be unstable. At the beginning of the year you will experience financial growth, but in the second half of the year cash flow is good only at the end of August and in September. The period from July to December mostly means financial expenditure connected to either business or family needs.

Love and family. Your personal life might be quite unpredictable.
If you begin a romantic affair in 2019, you can expect various problems at the end of the year. Serious emotional suffering is possible from June to December and you will need to consider your priorities. At the end of the year, you will have to come to a final decision although this might equally be made for you.

Couples might have some problems with children in the second half of the year. In the best-case scenario, your children's development just needs routine investment. In the worst-case scenario, you will have to spend the bulk of your family budget on solving their problems.

Many of you will want to solve housing problems. You may purchase a flat, a house, a country house. In some cases, this might be far away from your current home.

Closer to the end of the year you might plan to move to a new place – perhaps somewhere you have lived in or visited numerous times. It might happen at the end of December 2020 for the more active and driven amongst you, but in 2021 for those more reserved and cautious.

Health. As your energy levels are not high this year, you need to lead a balanced lifestyle and take proper care of yourself.

CAPRICORN

Jupiter is in Capricorn for the whole of 2020 and there is no better position for it. This powerful planet, in combination with Saturn and Pluto, brings new horizons and allows you to show yourself in the best possible light. Jupiter makes you almost invulnerable to problems and gives you the chance to achieve your ambitions both in work and in love.

Business. The first half of 2020 looks good. Many professionally active Capricorns will be on the crest of a wave in their career and will literally be able to move mountains in the three coming years.

Entrepreneurs and managers of all levels are likely to pursue promising new projects and lucrative deals.

Great opportunities open for clerical workers. You will find a new job. If you have recently got a new job, you will be able to strengthen your position there.

There is a saying, 'one cloud can darken the sun' and indeed the period from July to December will be unfavourable.

Entrepreneurs will face problems with property, land and larger premises. It is impossible to give a general forecast as this varies from case to case;

in the best-case scenario, you merely have to re-organise your business; in the worst-case, you have to defend your legal rights to your own business. Jumping ahead, we can say that you will be on the winning side, but that it will be a long, hard fight.

Clerical workers will experience major change in their company but despite the ensuing problems and stress, you will come out on top.

Money. The financial situation for most Capricorns is quite stable. If you want to be generous, you can be; but it is fine to just hang on to what you have. Any problems in the second half of the year will not be of a financial nature and you will not have to ask for money.

Love and family. In romantic relationships or in family life, you will need to make a few serious decisions.

In some situations, you will face a difficult choice between love and obligation. You should remember that it is very difficult to successfully have a foot in two camps. The advice of the astrologer is to get off the fence and choose one thing or the other.

Unhappy couples might be very close to divorce and the dividing up of property. Disagreements might continue for the second half of the year, and only by the end of December will you be able to reach a compromise. The situation will be even worse if the spouses own a business, although you will eventually get through it.

In all difficult situations, your children will be supportive. Moreover, their influence in the second half of the year will help you to reach a compromise or, in some cases, even to make up.

Health. Your energy levels are quite high in 2020, and you need not worry about illness.

AQUARIUS

2020 will be a difficult year with a lot of changes. The key thing is to change your old and tired ways and to plan for your future.

Business. In the first half of the year, many Aquarians will be busy with the preparation of new projects. Entrepreneurs and managers of all levels will do a good piece of property business and their business will expand. There will be, however, numerous issues connected to face in this period.

For clerical workers, the first half of the year is quite tranquil, although many of you start planning a job change; you will make it fly but only next year, in 2021.

The second part of the year is less tranquil. During this period, you will reconsider your plans and the situation will then start to look more realistic. Those whose interests are connected to partners from other cities and overseas will face serious problems. Overseas colleagues will behave in an aggressive manner and this will unsurprisingly cause tensions. The root of the problem might be property or land and the resulting, acute struggle will last from June to December 2020.

In other cases, there will be possible legal problems, inspections and checks; these will be difficult to resolve. However, by the end of 2021 you will reach a good compromise allowing you to escape any troubling circumstances.

Money. Financially, the first half of the year is stable. You may have income from different sources, and it will likely increase. Builders and those whose business is real estate or land will be especially successful.

Those not involved in business can rely on the support of parents, close friends and relatives. You might come into an inheritance or sell your property at a good price.

The second half of the year is less favourable and shows a decline in income and a growth in expenses. In some cases, it is connected to problems in business. In other cases, with troubles in your personal life.

Love and family. Many families might completely change their way of life. You may make a major renovation to your house or you may buy or sell a flat, a house or a country house. If you have such plans you should involve lawyers in order to comply with the letter of the law; otherwise you will have to deal with extended problems.

Those who own property abroad should also be cautious. In the second part of the year, international tensions might put your ownership of the property into question.

You might be involved in a spate of conflicts with your relatives. There might also be a long conflict with a particular relative, or a difficult situation with a close friend.

For romantic affairs this year is neutral with nothing extraordinary forecast to happen.

However, if the person you love lives abroad, you will face problems in the second half of the year that will not finish before December.

Health. Your energy levels are not high in 2020 and for this reason you should take care of yourself and keep to your limits. It is possible that you will have to take care of some family members; try to consider all possible options and take any necessary steps in advance. In the second part of the year, you should also be more careful while driving, as the chances of accidents and injuries are quite high.

PISCES

2020 opens up all sorts of new opportunities but these may also become extra problems that require your time and money to resolve. Nothing can be done about it - it's just the way of the world.

Business. In the first half of the year, you will be supported by high-powered friends and more recent high-flying acquaintances. At the beginning your business relationships will develop well; there is a good possibility of new project and financial successes, of meeting many interesting people and increasing your influence and popularity. New colleagues and old friends will set you new tasks but also provide the facilities for development; you will cope with everything brilliantly.
In the second half of the year, however, in June, your luck will turn, and you will notice the first dark clouds on the horizon - inevitably followed by the storm! You will be confronted with financial disagreements that

may be long-term and almost intractable. The problem may snowball into to a very serious argument where you might even lose some assets, but you will be able to weather the storm.

Money. Financially, 2020 is quite changeable. If in the first half of the year, you can expect a healthy income and can trust in your luck, while the second half of the year is financially challenging. In some cases, this is connected to work; in other cases, to your personal life.

Love and family. The first half of the year is a fortunate time for romantic relationships and personal life. Lady Luck will smile on those who have long been seeking a soulmate. You will meet a lot of new people and the love of your life could possibly be among them. It is possible that your lover will live in a different city or even abroad and so you may have to travel a lot.

However, those who already in a romantic relationship might have a difficult choice to make. In such a situation, Pisceans are likely to have disagreements about joint property and parenting - this is especially true for the second half of the year.

Strong couples may have problems with children, and in some cases, this will require quite serious expenditure.

For family relationships and romantic affairs, the second half of the year is the most difficult time and many relationships will be tested for strength.

Health. Your energy levels are quite high in 2020 and there is no need to worry about your health.

JANUARY

ARIES

In January, you remain fully in control. Everything goes smoothly and there is no turning back!

Business. Your professional activity levels in January will be quite high and perhaps even ahead of the curve. The winter holidays will not be an issue and you will still make progress. Almost all those of your birth sign will succeed this month. If you have a nagging feeling that something should be changed in your work, January is the best time to make such changes.

Entrepreneurs will reap a very good return from all their work of recent months. They will also conceive of new and grand projects and there will be good opportunities for these to come to fruition.

Clerical workers might expect either a good promotion, or a job offer in a new place.

Relationships with colleagues from other cities and overseas become more intense. You might have a very successful business trip.

Relationships with management, friends and sponsors will improve markedly. If you need to ask for help and assistance, you will receive it.

Money. When the professional situation is so favourable, there will not be any financial problems. Your assets will increase, and this is true for both businessmen and clerical workers. Expenses are not huge, and most of them are to be expected in the last twenty days of January.

Love and family. This month your personal life fades into insignificance and becomes of little consequence when compared to your work. Nevertheless, you should not forget about your family members completely for they will certainly still need your care and attention. If you concentrate solely on work and become distant and hard to reach, you will inevitably face misunderstanding, conflict and arguments at the end of the month.

During the period from January 26th to 30th, Mars and Venus are on hostile terms. This means that your partner or others close to you may pursue any legitimate grievances that they have with you. You should remember this, try not to be too self-centred and show respect for those whom you love.

Health. Your energy levels are high in January and you there is no reason for you to worry about your health. Only in the last ten days of January should you be careful during trips and while driving.

TAURUS

Renewal is the main theme of January. For some of you this means taking a path to a different future, for others it means taking long-distance trips.

Business. Most of January is perfect for planning and working out projects connected with long-distance travel to other cities and abroad. You are likely to have a successful trip where meeting old friends and partners can lucratively renew former business relationships.

Entrepreneurs will be able to turn over a new leaf; probably far from their home.

Clerical workers will have a good chance of changing jobs or getting a promotion.
January is the perfect time to learn something new and to find new approaches. If you want to study in a different city or abroad, you should go for it. You are on a roll!

Money. The financial situation this month is unpredictable; money will come and go. In some cases, your expenses are connected to your trips, in other cases to efforts to renew your lifestyle.

You might expect to receive small amounts of money on the 7th, 8th and 22nd – 25th of January.

At the same time, you will have to repay debts and loans. Mars is aggressive and it warns you to be cautious with any assets in your care; there is a good chance of unexpected loss and theft this month.

Love and family. January will be romantic. Some Taureans will hear the calling of their love and travel long distances to be with them - this is not new or unexpected. You might even move to be with someone you have known for a long time.

Those with families might also make a move to a different city or abroad in search of a brighter future. For some of you it might be either a new flat or house or the renovation of your current property.

Married couples and those in romantic relationships will travel to see old friends and relatives.

It is possible that January reveals a hidden, and in most cases brighter, side of the character of some people you have known for a long time.

Those who do not have a long-term partner can expect to meet their future soulmate; probably someone who has come from afar.

Health. Your energy levels are quite high in January, but there is a danger of accidents and injuries. Those fond of extreme sports and fast driving should bear this in mind.

GEMINI

January is time to resolve some serious issues that have been bothering you for a while. By seeing the problem from a new perspective, you gain understanding of how to deal with it.

Go for it! You are on the right path.

Business. Quite a difficult and important period is coming your way. Entrepreneurs and managers will realise the pressing need for fundamental change in their business and begin to make these changes.

Business partners will not only encourage you during this period but will support you financially in all activities. When discussing the terms of future business and when drawing up contracts, you should pay close attention to the devil in the detail – this might mean involving lawyers in order to avoid any ambiguity. Even if you trust your partners and consider them reliable, you should remember the well-known saying, 'better safe than sorry'. Clerical workers should also follow this advice if they decide to change their place of work.

Money. There are unlikely to be any problems with your finances in January. Your partners will open a reasonable credit line for you possibly with very good terms. You might buy or sell property at a good price.

Those not involved in business, will receive support from parents and close friends. There is the possibility of coming into an inheritance.

Love and family. January is a time of serious change in your personal life. Families and those who have not yet met their soulmate will start setting up home. Some people will start looking for new accommodation, others will start major repairs and renovation. There will be no money problems with this; either your parents or somebody you know well will lend you the money. If you do decide to take out a loan, the terms will be favourable.

Your relationship with your partner might occasionally become tense. It is possible that your partner will start being very direct about what they expect from your relationship. You should accept and welcome this as it will subsequently give you the chance to stand up to your partner.
If you plan an addition to your family, January is a good time for this.

Health. Your energy levels are not high in January - you need to take care of yourself and to keep everything within limits. Those who have old musculoskeletal problems or who suffer from arthrosis or arthritis should be extra careful.

There is a high chance of injuries and accidents so you should avoid risky situations and be careful and cautious. These recommendations are valid for the whole month but particularly on the full-moon days of January 9th to 11th.

CANCER

In January your plans receive support and your dreams might come true. This may be hard to believe this as things have not been good for a while, but the stars are on your side now and you should start to believe in your coming good fortune.

Business. January is a time for active communication and co-operation. You might be surrounded by new partners, former colleagues, and those with power and money; their support will help you to resolve any past problems and make for a better future. This is true for all Cancerians, but mainly for those who have outstanding legal issues or who face the consequences of the actions of government institutions. The time has come to fix these problems and you can ask your partners and colleagues for help without hesitation as you will be heard and understood correctly.

Your relations with colleagues from other cities and overseas are developing well. You might have a lucrative business trip, meet new partners or sign new contracts that give the future a bright outlook.

Money. Although your professional competence is growing, your financial situation will not change in the first twenty days of January.

The situation will improve after the new moon on January 24th when you can rely on the support of your business partners or close friends and relatives. The financial situation might change for the better in the last ten days of the month or in February.

Love and family. January is a time for romance. Single people will meet somebody interesting and there is a good chance that this affair will grow into marriage. Your current relationship might improve. Couples who have split up as a result of arguments, misunderstandings or distance might reconsider and begin thinking about getting back together. Go for it! You should remember that this is a unique opportunity to change your life and that you will not have such a possibility in the second part of the year.

Trips that you have planned for January will be successful. Every evening of this romantic month is perfect for dating or for heart-to-heart talks.

The active period for relationships in January is from the 1st to the 24th. The last ten days of this month are better for tranquil reflection on the events; it is worth having a break from people and fresh experiences.

Health. Your energy levels are quite high in the first twenty days of the month, and you should not worry about your health.

Nevertheless, it is always wise to take care of your health and the stars recommend paying extra attention to your digestive system. After the New moon, on the 24th of January, your energy levels will fall dramatically, and so you should take extra care of yourself.

LEO

In January, you will become a true cart horse and your productivity will be very high. The discipline and determination which are characteristic of you this month will move mountains.

Business. As soon as the Christmas holidays are finished, you should leap into action. Entrepreneurs and managers will launch a project that attracts the full support of their employees - their help will underpin the project and be most useful. Via strenuous efforts, you will sort out numerous problems and your business will move ahead.

Clerical workers will have a brilliant chance to show their talents to their full extent - this is especially important for those who have recently been promoted or have changed job.

Those who have been unemployed for a long time can expect to find employment in January.

Your partnership with colleagues from other cities and overseas is developing well and you might have to go on a business trip.

Money. Solid professional achievements will lead to increased cash flow. The approximate dates for receipt of large sums of money in January are the 5th,6th,14th,15th,22nd and 23rd.

There will not be many expenses this month; money will mainly be spent on your children and relatives.

Love and family. Everything is quiet and predictable in your personal life. Married couples will spend lots of time with their children. The children will not be a cause for concern to their parents.
The last ten days of the month are not good for romantic relations. You might expect serious misunderstandings and arguments in the period from the 25th to the 30th of January - these might be financial disagreements or complaints about lack of attention.

Looking further forward, we can say that these problems will repeat themselves later on in the year. This is why it is worth getting everything out into the open now; no matter how difficult and unpleasant it might be. It looks like the time has come to dot the 'I's and cross the 'T's.
Health. Your energy levels are not high in January. Therefore, you should take care of yourself and protect your body from colds and infections. The elderly and those with musculoskeletal problems should be especially cautious.

The most difficult period in January, when you might notice lowered energy levels, is from the 9th to the 12th. However, January is the perfect time to start sports, various diets, massage and other recreational activities. If you give it a go this month, you have a good chance to come across a beneficial routine.

VIRGO

The Christmas holidays might have tired you - you cannot

*wait until they finally finish - but start to do something use-
ful and important. For instance, put your household in order.*

Business. Most of January will be devoted to family and personal affairs
and you will be able to fully dedicate yourself to work only in the last ten
days of January or even a bit later. In January, you will be dreaming about
making big changes at work and to your lifestyle. You should be cautious,
however while trying to make those dreams come true as it is possible that
not all your dreams are so well-thought out and that not all the people
whom you trust are so reliable.

Your partnership with colleagues from other cities and overseas is developing well; you might have a very successful business trip at the beginning
of the month.

Any difficult relations with your business partners are coming to a resolution. In the near future, you will be able to banish the doubts which were
characteristic of 2019 and build a genuine partnership.

Money. Despite the improving business situation, you are likely to have
financial problems. You will spend lots of money on the needs of your
family or on property renovation. You may expect small amounts of money – really just chicken feed - on the 7th, 8th, 16th, 17th, 25th and 26th of
January.

The luckiest of your birth sign might expect all sorts of prizes and pay-
offs - maybe you should buy a lottery ticket or try your luck at the betting
shop or casino.

Love and family. When choosing between family and business this
month, you should prioritize your family; your nearest and dearest need
you. Many of your sign will focus on their children and do everything to
further their welfare and well-being. These efforts will pay off - your kids
will do just great!

Some of your sign will start renovating their homes or move to new accommodation.

January is an excellent time for those who are in love and your relationship will noticeably improve. You might travel together and have fresh and

stimulating experiences that impact positively on your relationship. The first twenty days are good for married couples and lovers. At the end of January, from the 25th to the 30th, however, you might have some arguments and disagreements.

You might go back to old friends or rekindle your relationship with an old flame. In general, you will have fun. Single people will meet somebody extraordinary and have a whirlwind romance.

In many families, there is a strong possibility of an addition to the family. There is a good chance of conception this month; either naturally or via fertility treatment.

Health. Your energy levels are quite high this month, and you should not have any concerns about your health.

LIBRA

You should take it slowly but remain in total control of events. Things at work and in your personal life are about to change - positively.

Business. You will be busy resolving family matters for most of January. Only the more incurable workaholics among you will start reorganising their business and this is likely to involve your business premises and land. Make sure that you conduct any deals correctly from legal point of view. Your efforts will yield positive results this time and you will get your reward - a good stepping-stone to a tremendous future.

Relations with colleagues from other cities and overseas are not stable. At the beginning of the month, you might have some misunderstandings and closer to the end of the month you are likely to have a serious conflict. However, it is nothing extraordinary and will do no harm to your business or your business relationships in the long run.

Another possible issue in January is your relationship with your colleagues and employees. Not all of your staff are competent and responsible unfortunately. Even though you have dealt with these same problems many

9

times before, this time you need to finally sort it out once and for all.

Money. Financially, the situation is stable and positive. You might get cash from various real estate deals and from your business partners. Those not involved in business might expect financial help from close relatives or parents and there is the possibility of coming into an inheritance.

Now is a good time to obtain a highly favourable loan.

Expenses are predictable and reasonable this month.

Love and family. In January, many Librans will be busy with family matters. It is time to change your way of life and routine: to equip your accommodation with new services and utilities; to renovate your house; to purchase new furniture. All these activities will go smoothly, and you might even decide to start a family business or to expand your current business.

Your relationships with your children are good as all problems and tensions have finally come to an end.

Those who are in love will decide to live together and can rely on help from their parents.

Relations with relatives will be strained and there might be a minor conflict in the last ten days of the month.

Health. Your energy levels are not high in January, but it will not lead to any serious illness if you stick to a healthy lifestyle. You do tend to gain weight, so it is worth starting to do some sport and keeping to a balanced diet.

SCORPIO

You will retain your positivity and self-belief for a long time to come yet. There is good reason for this, so keep it up!

Business. The main trend for January is the development of your partnerships with colleagues from other cities and overseas. Events that take place in January might reshape your life, and in some cases, even lead to moving to a new place. All these changes are for the best so don't fret – just follow your chosen path.

You will resume relations with old colleagues and friends who live far away. You might meet new partners with whom you are likely to build strong relationships.

January is a great time to start learning and to develop your creativity. If you plan to learn something new in a different city or abroad, it is the perfect time.

All the trips you plan for January will be successful ones.

Money. The financial situation is stable, and you will have a regular inflow of cash. Only at the end of the month might you have extra expenses connected with close relatives or children.

Love and family. You might face changes in your family life. Relationships with relatives become more important and their influence on various aspects of your life significant. You should remember that you can move mountains with the help of your close relatives.

Many families will make the decision to move house and will take the first steps towards this in January.

Relations between lovers become complicated, they might expect some serious arguments in the final ten days of the month. The reason for these disagreements is your differing outlook on life, differing values or, sadly, money.

You should remember that taking care of your partner entails real deeds. Be generous! This piece of advice is especially true for men, but women should also pay heed to this. Life offers up many challenges and if your partner needs help, you should be there for them.

Families might have problems with their children and it is likely that it will take money to resolve. Kids are kids. Who else will help them if not you?

Health. Your energy levels are really high in January. All you need do is steer your energy in the right direction.

SAGITTARIUS

Wisdom and a broad mind open new horizons for you - both professionally and financially. In fact, this is a new level and a different future.

Business. There is a good possibility that all your ambitions, even if they seem bold and impossible, will come true this month. Entrepreneurs might expect major projects to come their way, with earnings like never before
.

Clerical workers might get a promotion with a serious salary increase. If you have already been promoted, you can expect to consolidate your position along with a raise.

During this month you are goal-oriented, self-confident and determined and everybody you deal with notices this.

Your relationships with colleagues from other cities and overseas are developing well - you might have a successful business trip. The best time for all business activity is the middle ten days of the month and here you can expect important business events.

Money. January is the best financial period in the last 10 years. Many Sagittarians will get a windfall. You will reach new financial heights and then be able to remain there for some time to come. The stars support you in all your plans and ambitions - you deserve it.

The biggest influx of money is expected in the last twenty days of the month.

Love and family. Things are about to change in your personal life and this is mostly connected to your finances. Many of your birth sign will have had ideas on how to improve your life and some of these plans will come to fruition this month. There might be big budget purchases this month - a house, a country house or a flat. In some cases, these purchases will be far from your current home.

Married couples might have disagreements about this, however. At the end of January these disagreements could lead to a serious conflict. Mars is in your birth sign all month and gives you plenty of energy. If you use this energy for peaceful purposes, you will not have any troubles.

Health. You are in good health in January - full of energy and ready to go. A slight lowering of your energy levels is possible during the period of the full moon from January 9th to 11th. For the rest of the time you will be like a whirlwind; in perpetual motion.

CAPRICORN

You are determined, motivated and self-confident in January. You know very well that you can achieve your goals. People around will look at you with admiration and even envy.

Business. It is unlikely that you will be idle during the Christmas holidays. You will spend most of the month working; you have many ideas and know exactly how to bring them to life. You will be able to find new approaches and possibly to change your relationships with business partners.

Your ties with colleagues from other cities and overseas will become more predictable. You might have a business trip in the first twenty days of the month where you reach agreement on many important issues.

The last ten days of January are less successful. Your colleagues might raise issues and doubts, but you will be able to deal with the situation and set the rules.

Money. Venus is responsible for your finances in most of January and this means that you should not expect any money problems. Your income will be regular. The approximate dates to receive large sums of money in January are the 3rd, 7th, 8th, 15th to 17th and 24th to 26th. Besides this, you can also expect some presents and other pleasant surprises; everything looks good!

Love and family. In your personal life everything also goes well. You are the centre of attention and all kinds of possibilities come your way. There is a strong possibility of adventure; you are feeling positive and longing for change but this might push you into unexpected or even risky actions, however. Some of you might have a non-committal romantic affair. Others will remain obsessed with someone you have been after for a long time.

This all seems rather good. But if you are in a relationship, a new affair might cause serious problems. You should remember the old saying, 'What is done in the dark eventually comes to light'. If you are no longer interested in your partner, however, this might not be so relevant.
Your relationship with your relatives will be clearer as you have been doing your best to clarify them. Closer to the end of the month, you are likely to have further disagreements, but there is still hope that you can overcome any misunderstandings.

Your relationship with your children is improving. In many families there is a good possibility of having a baby. If you are planning IVF, there is good chance of success.

Health. You are in good health and extremely attractive in January - many will notice you.

You should be careful while traveling and driving between the 25th and 30th of January.

AQUARIUS

January is downtime. The stars recommend that you start saving your energy and limiting yourself to safe, routine activity.

Business. The Christmas holiday must have had a relaxing effect on you. This is not a bad period for you, but starting any serious deals is not recommended - the best you can hope for is to get your ducks in a row and to weigh up your future actions.

Entrepreneurs and managers will start changing their business and this might be the expansion of a business or laying the groundwork for further business development.

You might enter into various property deals; either an advantageous purchase or a profitable sale.

You might move your business to a different city or just to new premises. Your relations with partners are harmonious, but closer to the end of the month financial disagreements become possible.

Clerical workers may have to face changes in their company - such as a change in management or redeployment - that push you to change your job and to look elsewhere to use your skills. You will definitely find such a place, if not this month then later.

Money. The financial situation is stable, and you will have regular income; not necessarily from your main job. You might make a profit from real estate. You are likely to get good terms on a loan or savings.

If you are not involved in business, you might get help from your parents or partner. You might come into an inheritance. At the end of the month, you might expect heavy expenses connected to your personal life or to your friends and business partners.

Family and love. In most cases, all the key events will take place within your family and your home. You might expect serious changes connected to property - either buying, selling or renovating your home. Some of your birth sign will do this in January, others in other months of 2020.

Family relations are quite balanced. Strong couples, being wise and loving, will overcome various domestic problems together.

Couples in a romantic relationship might face some difficulties in the last ten days of January. They might have misunderstandings and arguments due to differing views on life and, which is maybe worse, financial problems. However, it should be said that all these problems can be sorted out if there is the mutual desire to do so.

Health. Your energy levels are not high in January. There are unfavourable days on the full moon days of the 9th to the 11th, and also the 22nd to the 25th. During these periods you should take more care of yourself and keep strictly to your limits. You should be careful when driving and avoid dangerous situations.

pisces

January is favourable. You are everybody's favourite, and this will impact your working and personal relationships.

Business. 'A friend at court is better than a penny in your purse' – this old piece of wisdom will come to your mind a few times in January. You will be surrounded by serious, strong people with power and money, and their influence on your professional activities will be surprisingly favourable. They are likely to support your ideas, to cushion you and to give you serious financial support.

You will meet new business partners quite unexpectedly; old friends will get back to you with invaluable offers of help; new partners from other cities and overseas will turn out to be very interesting, useful and beneficial. To cut a long story short, from all the possibilities which January offers, you will need to choose those that will best lead you to success. This is an ideal moment in your life, and you should not let it pass you by.

Money. Despite your obvious professional success, you should be careful in financial matters. This does not mean that you will be short of money, but your costs in January might be excessive. Indeed, some of your sign might be tempted to splash out, leading inevitably to a serious hole in your budget come the end of January.

Love and family. You will show off your bright and creative side in January. This will attract people to you like moths to a flame and your soulmate might well be amongst them. It is possible that you meet your future partner during a trip or amongst friends who have come from afar. In other words, the possibility of a sparkling romance this month is high. If you are already in a relationship, a new affair will bring serious problems, but these will not manifest themselves until later in the year.

Relations with your relatives will improve and you might renew contact with those from other cities or abroad. Any trips that you have planned for January will be successful, especially for married couples and lovers.

Health. Your energy levels are high this month and you should not worry about your health.

FEBRUARY

ARIES

You are on the threshold of a successful period in your life when everything goes according to plan. Without a doubt you are a leader, but you can now rely on your friends.

Business. The best time for all professionals is from the 1st to the 17th of February. During this time, you will attract support from your friends or people who have money and power. Relationships with partners from other cities and overseas are developing well and all past misunderstandings will be successfully resolved.

The second half of the month is neither so good nor so dynamic, however. During this period, you will have to realise that all the activities you have planned need better organisation and more careful planning. You will be busy doing this not only in the second half of February but also in March.

If you have a suspicion that something should be changed in your work, now is the best time to do so; this does not necessarily mean changing your place of work. There is a good chance of finding new approaches to work and of correcting any defects which your projects may have. Managers should watch their employees and colleagues because there is a good possibility of underhanded activity.

It is also possible that your team is not yet ready for ambitious future projects - you will have to admit this to yourself and take the required steps to resolve this situation. Mercury is moving in the opposite direction and new people might turn out to be unreliable and unprofessional. There-fore, the stars do not advise you to employ new people in the period from the 17th of February to the 10th of March. You would eventually under-stand that they were of no use and only caused extra problems.

Money. You are unlikely to have financial problems as there will be regu-lar and decent income. You will also have some expenses connected to the development of your business or your family.

Love and family. In the first twenty days of February, you are sociable and inquisitive, charming and attractive – many different people are certain to find these characteristics attractive.

New contacts and dates are likely to happen in the second half of the month. You might also have a trip where you can mix business with pleas-ure; having a great time while establishing new and useful business con-tacts.

There is the possibility of an affair, but it is unlikely to be a watershed moment in your life. If you are feeling lonely or disappointed, however, it may not be such a bad thing.

If you are in a long-term relationship with a partner, you should remem-ber that the truth will out, and so you should behave yourself. Secrets are likely to be revealed at the end of February or in March, and so it would be wise to be circumspect and not hurt those about whom you genuinely care. Married couples should spend quality time with their children for this will make everybody happy.

Health. Your energy levels are quite high in the first twenty days of Feb-ruary and there is no need to worry about your health. In the last ten days of February your energy levels might fall away some, but this does not indicate any serious health problems.

TAURUS

Wisdom and open-mindedness open new doors for you.

Changes are on the horizon.

Business. February, at least the first half, is an ideal time to start a new business, to land a lucrative contract or to discuss future co-operation with partners.
Clerical workers have a good chance of finding a more interesting and rewarding job with good prospects.

It is possible that friends or some important people will play a major role in your dealings this month. In the first half of the month, your relationships will develop in the best possible way. However, in the second half of the month you will start to notice some worrying patterns.

People on whom you have previously relied will, for various reasons, take a more neutral attitude towards you. In some cases, a deal will drag on because your partners have over-estimated their abilities. In other cases, they will change their mind about helping you or the circumstances might have simply changed. It is also likely that the main reason is a financial disagreement and you will need to decide what to do about this.

Relationships with your colleagues from other cities and overseas are still very important, and in this area, business looks quite positive.

Money. The financial situation will improve slightly. The approximate dates in February for receiving large amounts of cash are the 4th, 5th, 12th, 13th, 21st and 22nd. On the other hand, many of your birth sign will need to repay loans or spend money on home improvements. In other words, the financial situation is not yet stable.

Love and family. You can feel the wind of change in your personal life. Some people will decide to move to a new place. In some cases, this is because of a partner who lives in a different city or abroad. In other cases, the reason for moving house might be relatives, old friends or a new job. Many families will move to a new flat or house or will finish furnishing a new home.
You need to be diplomatic and careful in your relations with your children. They might have some issues in the period from the 17th of February to the 10th of March and you must give them the necessary support; both moral and financial.

This period might be difficult for couples. They will face some misunderstandings, and it is better not to bury things but to discuss them openly with care and tact - this is particularly true for financial issues. Money and love do not always match, and you need to remember this.

Health. Your energy levels are quite high in February and there is no need to worry about your health.

GEMINI

February is a month of contrasts for Gemini. The first half is
light while the second half appears darker.

Business. It is safe to say that the period from the 1st to the 17th of February is positive. Both meeting new partners and negotiations will be useful and agreeable. There will be renewal of your relationships with colleagues from other cities and overseas. There is a good possibility of either making a business trip or having your long-distance partners visit you and offering new ways of co-operation.

Your protector - Mercury - starts to move backwards in the second half of the month and so this period is not so dynamic; you will notice that pace of development in your professional life begins to slow. You therefore need to go back to some issues that you thought had been sorted out - some things will have to be finished, and other things changed.

Entrepreneurs and managers will continue the reorganisation of their business and will invite their partners to join the reorganisation process. The partners will certainly be of big help in word and deed.

Clerical workers will carry out a large number of different tasks. At first sight they will seem mundane, but in reality, this work is very important. However, do not be upset if things do not go smoothly at first and if you cannot do it yourself, reach out to those who can help. Even if things don't change immediately, you will eventually get your own way.

Money. The financial situation is stable, and you will have regular cash flow. You can expect the biggest amounts of money on the 6th, 14th, 15th and 23 - 25th of February.

Besides your own earnings, you can rely on the support of your parents or your partner. You will not have many costs and they will all be predictable and reasonable.

Love and family. Everything goes well in your personal life. Happy families and recently reunited lovers will continue furnishing their homes with varying degrees of success.

Many Gemini will be scrambling between family and work. You should be careful not to lose something very important and this is especially relevant for those who plan to move to a different city or a new property.

Single people will make new acquaintances, but it is more likely to be a quick fling rather than anything more serious. It might happen during a trip or with someone who has travelled from a long way away.

Health. Your energy levels will grow remarkably this month, and you will avoid any health problems.

CANCER

Being wise and open-minded may open new doors for you; especially if you remember the old saying, 'no man is an island'.

Business. The first half of the month is a reasonable and quite predictable period. You can expect support from your business partners and to meet new people who may turn out to be both interesting and quite powerful. Entrepreneurs and managers will be busy discussing financial plans, such as capital and other financial injections into a joint business; these questions will definitely be solved, but only after much debate.

Clerical workers will have a quiet period with neither achievements nor troubles. Many of your birth sign will want to take a break and go to the seaside to enjoy some sunny weather. Those who stay at work should be attentive to their duties, especially during the second half of the month.

During this period, you might be faced with business difficulties such as paperwork and red tape.

Those who have legal problems should be extra careful with documentation. It is also worth paying more attention to the work of your lawyers; this will help you to avoid many problems either now or in future. Your relations with colleagues from other cities and overseas are developing well, although in the second half of the month you should be cautious and pay more attention to detail.

Money. The financial situation is generally stable, but this mainly concerns the finances of your business rather than your own income. You might receive the reimbursement of an old debt or get a loan on easy terms.

You might have to deal with numerous costs, but these are organizational costs and so they are expected. Those in romantic relationships can expect support from a more prosperous partner.

Love and family. Everything is well and quiet in your personal life. Married couples who have recently made up can enjoy a happy family life or perhaps go on a second honeymoon somewhere far from home.

Long-term lovers will have a similar period in their lives. Single people might see an old friend from a new angle - you will be surprised that you hadn't noticed such a diamond right there next to you. Even if you have doubts in the second half of the month, you should not worry - love is in the air.

Health. Your energy levels are not high in the first twenty days of February and you might feel lethargic, tired and lazy.
You can expect a burst of energy after the new moon on the 24th of February and you will feel happier, more cheerful and confident after this.

LEO

Discipline, determination and ambition will help you to achieve your goals. Even if you don't get full credit for your achievements, you can nevertheless be proud of what you have done.

Business. You will see new prospects in the first ten days of February and future opportunities look impressive; all you need do is find a way to turn them into reality. Entrepreneurs and managers of different levels will be busy working at such projects. You will definitely see positive results but probably not quite as rapidly as you had hoped. In the second half of the month, you will probably start to see delays in your business caused by red tape, collecting the necessary paperwork and finding the appropriate contacts to assist you. This is why you should postpone the most important business activities to the first ten days in March - also an excellent time for meeting the right people.

Clerical workers will have additional responsibilities, and the stars see this as a very useful opportunity for the future as you might get promoted as a result and get a salary increase. Even if it means working day and night, your hard work will pay you back.

Money. The financial situation is generally stable. Apart from regular earnings, you can rely on loans and even the support of government institutions.

Those who are not involved in business can expect help from parents or close relatives. Some Leos can expect such help in the first half of February, others in the second half of March.

Love and family. Your life is full of routine domestic concerns. In some cases, this involves children and it is possible that a substantial part of your family budget will be spent on finishing and furnishing the house of an adult child, or possibly on their other needs.

February is a good month for those who are in love, especially if you have mutual professional interests and if there are no financial misunderstandings.

This year predicts a so-called office romance and if new colleagues turn up in the office before the 17th of February, there might be mutual interest. However, if new people appear in your life in the period from the 17th of February to the 10th of March, they will bring no joy, only problems.

Nevertheless, this is a good time to renew old friendships and see people you haven't got together with for a long time.

Health. Your energy levels are not high in February, but you should not have to worry about your health as long as you keep to your limits. Those who have a long-standing problem with their musculoskeletal system or who suffer from arthritis or arthrosis need to be extra cautious.

VIRGO

This month starts positively and the more you work put in,
the better the results.

Business. The first half of February is the best time for professional activities. During this period, you will exude serenity, optimism and self-confidence and with such an outlook, your success is assured. Negotiations, meeting new people and co-operation with colleagues from other cities and overseas all bode well for the future. There is a high possibility of business trips in the early part of February.

Planned changes to your business become more realistic and formed and you will reach your goal soon enough.
Those planning partnerships with long-distance colleagues will have to move to a new location; this is another step forward and will be a success. The second half of February looks less positive, however. You will have to improve your projects and make necessary adjustments. The stable position of your partners may change, and although you may have to prove the reliability and profitability of your business, there is good reason to believe that you will succeed. All you need do is concentrate your attention on the main things and to act without undue haste. You should remember that to rush at this time is to make a mistake.

Money. The financial situation is not stable, but everything that you do now will bring good profit in the near future. So, you need to work at it and believe that everything will turn out fine.

You can still expect a small inflow of cash in February. The approximate dates for this are the 4th, 5th, 12th, 13th, 28th and 29th.

Love and family. Your personal life comes to the fore in February. Many under your birth sign will be busy helping your children and you will do almost anything to guarantee them a happy future.

Romantic relations are quite stable in the first half of the month, but in the second half of the month they do become somewhat fraught. You should not expect anything major; just a few minor misunderstandings and disagreements.

There is a good chance of a trip at the beginning or the end of the month and this will relieve any pressure pent up in your relationship.

Health. Your energy levels are quite high and there is no need to worry about your health. February is a good time to pay attention to your health and to your appearance. A sauna, a massage, a trip to the beauty salon and other similar activities will be good not only for your body, but also for your soul.

LIBRA

This month is mostly quite positive. You will take part in various meetings, negotiations and presentations and the outstanding results make you a popular person. Good luck!

Business. The first half of February is a positive and creative period. Give rein to your imagination and inventiveness and don't be afraid to use more unconventional methods in your work. Those who are involved in the construction business, or who work with land and real estate will be especially successful.

Entrepreneurs and managers are still busy working at the reorganisation and expansion of their business and they will soon have every right to be proud of their achievements.

Relationships with your colleagues from other cities and overseas are quite contrary, but the situation will continue to improve, albeit slowly. It will take time to resolve all of the disputes, but you know deep down that major deals cannot be closed overnight.

The second part of the month is not quite as positive. You will face delays in business projects from the need to adjust your plans and work further on some important documents.

Entrepreneurs will have problems with employees who turn out to be careless and incompetent. After having put things right in this vital area, your business will develop far better than before.

Clerical workers are likely to have problems with colleagues that possibly include disagreements and underhand deals. In such a case, you should not hustle but take one step at a time and carry on with your duties properly.

Money. The financial situation is stable but nothing more. You can't expect great progress in this area at the moment, but those whose business is connected with land and property might make quite a profit this month. Additional income is possible if you rent or sell your flat, house, or country house.

Love and family. You can expect a powerful renewal process in your personal life. Primarily, it will affect your daily routine. Your home upgrade is going well in terms of either buying new accommodation or completely refurbishing your present home. It is also possible that married couples will start a joint activity connected either to land or construction and real estate.

Your relationships with your children will improve, largely because you will have more time to spend with them. In the second part of the month, you will need to be more careful with the younger generation; try to be more involved in their problems and help them with word and deed.

Your relations with your relatives are complicated; there will not be any major conflicts, but some low level misunderstandings are possible.

The second half of the month is difficult for romantic relationships, and you may notice darker clouds looming on the horizon. Even if the circumstances do not seem entirely favourable, there is no cause for concern. You should remember the old saying, 'a quarrel between lovers is merely the renewal of their love' - time will pass and the clouds will clear soon enough.

Health. Your energy levels are sufficiently high this month not to have to worry about your health.

SCORPIO

Discipline, reserve and accuracy are the necessary qualities for you in February. Firstly, these will help you to resolve your problems. Secondly, you will be able to avoid the hustle and bustle.

Business. For most of February, entrepreneurs and managers will be occupied with various economic and organisational matters and these are likely to include a staff reshuffle, renovation of your premises and real estate activities.

Those planning to start a business in a different city or abroad can go ahead and start this project now. In the first half of the month, things go well, but the second half of the month looks less positive and progressive. You will have to face various delays and problems with either red tape, a lack of professional staff or other drawbacks and it will take at least a month to sort these out. However, there is nothing out of the ordinary and you will start to successfully overcome the situation in the second half of the month.

Clerical workers will have a quiet month. You might have to take your holiday or take a few days off in order to spend time on family needs. Those who stay at work will be torn between work and family needs.

Money. The financial situation is stable, but only stable. There will be neither big gains nor losses in February. You can expect strong support from your relatives, parents and senior members of your family.

Love and family. You will spend a lot of February with your close family members but this does not necessarily mean problems. On the other hand, it is a good time to renovate your home, to improve your lifestyle and to deepen your family ties.

Your relationship with your relatives is still very important and the fact that they take a big part in your life is very positive. Some of your relatives will succeed in their business and this is very positive news for the family. Those who plan a long trip or to move house can expect help from both close and distant relatives.

You should pay more attention to your children. They are facing big changes in their lives, and it is essential that you stay close to them during this important period.

February is good for those in romantic relationships. In the first half of the month, you will notice development and an improvement in your relationship. The second part of the month will be quieter, but you might have a trip where a long-standing relationship takes on fresh colours. The period from the 17th of February to the 10th of March is an ideal time to pick up with old friends and old flames. If you plan to move to a new place, February is a good time to set up home in a different city or abroad.

Health. Your energy levels are quite high this month and there is no need to worry about your health.

SAGITTARIUS

You keep moving forward and, this time, you make the most of your ideas.

Business. You will spend most of February travelling and sorting out various urgent issues. The first half of the month will be very busy, and it will be difficult to stop you.

Entrepreneurs and managers will establish contacts with colleagues from other cities and overseas that have impact positively on their business. The first half of the month is most dynamic, and during this period you can move the proverbial mountain.

The second part of February is less active, but you will still be productive in sorting various economic problems, such as the construction or major renovation of your premises. You might face various delays and problems in the period from the 17th of February to the 10th of March, but this might prove to be a blessing as you now have the opportunity to more closely scrutinize your projects and make any necessary changes - you might even find original solutions and easier ways to implement your plans that you had previously missed.

Money. The financial situation is stable with an obvious upswing. You will have regular income and the approximate dates in February for the credit of large sums to your account are the 2nd ,3rd ,10th ,11th, 14th ,15th, the 19th to the 21st, the 28th and 29th

Love and family. Romantically, everything is quiet and smooth. People in love have balanced relations; they might go away together or plan such a trip in the near future.

Married couples will plan to renovate their house or maybe to buy a new flat, house, summer cabin or country house. Some Sagittarians will be able to fulfil such plans at various points in 2020. Others will make their plan reality later, but in the near future.

However, you should not rush and definitely not make any serious decisions in the period from the 17th of February to the 10th of March. Any family or economic activities you start during this time might fail although you may as well go on working on your plans - this is a good time to further elaborate on your plans, make necessary changes to documentation and generally improve the family climate.

Health. You are healthy and full of energy in February. All health problems will stay away.

CAPRICORN

You can really show your best side in February. Discipline, responsibility and reliability ensure success in all areas.

Business. The most important things this month are your work and career. The sky is the limit and you should devote yourself utterly to new opportunities, for example, if you have to leave for long-distance business trips, you should do so.

Complicated relations with colleagues from other cities and overseas will eventually settle down and it seems that after protracted disagreements, you will finally be able to do the impossible - to sort out all the problems and close the chapter. It will not happen immediately because you will have to revisit the same questions again in the second half of March in order to reconcile final issues. The best advice in this situation is to do everything yourself; only you will be able to succeed.

All the business trips you have planned for this period will go well, especially if they happen in the first half of the month.

Clerical workers might receive an offer they will not be able to turn down. You might have been waiting for this chance for a long time and the time has come!

Fortunate Capricorns can expect success this month. Others will have a sporting chance for future successes.

Money. The financial situation is stable. You will receive regular income and there is no need to worry about money.

Love and family. The renewal of your personal life continues. Determined Uranus is lodged in the love sector of the sky and this suggests that your present relationship has become stale and routine. This process did start not today, but it is gathering pace each and every day. Will it cause problems? For sure; and especially for couples where the partners continue to harbour the burden of old problems and resentments.

Might there, however, be someone more interesting for you than your present partner? This time the stars are on the side of a new relationship that could change your life. If your love is still strong, however, there are no threats to your relationship.

Strong couples will be busy with household and family activities. The younger generations might face some positive changes and you will contribute to this process both morally and financially.

The strained relations with your relatives, that have lately been of concern will improve. You will resolve the situation with a firm hand and your relatives will have to reluctantly admit that you were, in fact, right. Single people might expect to meet new people or rekindle romantic relations with a former lover. Many of your sign will plan trips that take place at the end of February or the beginning of March.

Health. You are healthy and full of energy in February, but the stars advise you to avoid hassles and to be cautious while driving in the period from the 17th of February to the 10th of March.

AQUARIUS

Events will allow you to see your life from a different angle.
Good luck!

Business. The first half of February is busy and dynamic. Entrepreneurs and managers will continue the revitalization of their business and possibly start looking for new space into which to expand.

Co-operation with partners from other cities and overseas is developing well and you might have a trip, lucrative negotiations or agreements to co-operate. Those involved in construction or the real estate business will have very good income, and all organizational problems will be successfully resolved.

Clerical workers will take an active part in corporate restructuring and your efforts will be noticed and duly appreciated.

The second part of the month does not look so good. Many problems, mainly financial issues, will be discussed at length but there is nothing extraordinary in this. Between the 17th of February and the 10th of March, you will have to weigh up all the possible variants and probably make changes to your current plans. After this, everything will slip into a better groove.

Money. The financial situation remains stable. Many of your birth sign will profit from real estate activities and some of you may come into an inheritance.
You might also expect financial support from your parents or family members.

Love and family. You are coming into a period of renewal in your personal life. For some it will affect your daily household routine, for others it will affect family matters.

In the first case, there is likely to be major refurbishment or renovation of your flat and perhaps even the purchase or sale of accommodation. In the second case, you will re-evaluate your family relationships.

In both cases you should not worry about the changes to come because they will drive you forward. This is also true for those who plan to move to a new city or abroad.

The stars advise you to be more cautious in executing real estate transactions, signing paperwork or transferring money in the period from the 17th of February to the 10th of March. The best tactics will be to analyse the situation and then to sign documents and transfer money only after the 10th of March. In this way you will avoid errors, deceit and losses.

Health. February is your month. Your energy levels will be high and all problems with health stay away from you.

pisces

New horizons open in front of you, but you need to be prepared. Most of February will be busy planning things. You cannot avoid this - great deeds take time.

Business. The main trend for this month is enhanced co-operation with colleagues from other cities and overseas. In the near future, you are likely to start a new project that will lead to changes that have a positive effect on your business. Your relationships with old friends or those in power might be also very important for business as the support of such people can help to resolve many problems. This is true for both clerical workers and entrepreneurs.

The first half of February is a predictable and positive period. However, the period from the 17th of February to the 10th of March will bring delays and problems. The future will prove that all these situations will be sorted out, but for now, the stars recommend stepping back, acting without undue haste and being moderate and diplomatic in your actions. It is possible that you will have to solve some disputes, make changes to documentation and then make your decision on a future project. Such necessary and important actions will help you to fully understand the changes and so make the right, balanced decision.

Money. The financial situation is stable although you should not expect any serious financial breakthroughs this month. This is more likely a matter for the near future, so you need to work hard and keep in mind that all your efforts will pay you back.

Love and family. In your personal life, February is also a time for change. Singles and those disappointed in a previous relationship might have a bright love affair. It is more likely that this time your lover will live in a different city or abroad. As a result, you might travel regularly or even move to a new place fairly soon.

Other couples might also move house and in some cases it will be related to relatives who live in a different city or abroad. In other cases, the reason for changing your place of residence will be either your or your partner's job.

All these important changes are only being prepared in February. The main events will happen either in March or during the summer of 2020.

Health. Your energy levels are not high this month, so you need to remember to rest, sleep and worry less. Everything will happen in its own time; there is no need to rush.

ARIES

'Slow and steady wins the race' – this should be your motto
for the month. It is true for both your work and personal life.

Business. In the first half of the month, you will have tons of things to do. You will make mistakes if you try to do things in a hurry, so under no circumstances should you rush or impose any deadlines upon yourself or others. You should begin by putting all your current problems into pigeonholes and starting to solve them prudently one by one. Don't be surprised if these endeavours take longer than you plan. The additional time is for you to work out any kinks - don't waste this time.

The stars still recommend entrepreneurs and managers to control employees and to check them regularly. This will help you to avoid many future problems. ,

Clerical workers should take into account that there may be people hostile to them amongst the staff. Any mistake you make now could lead to a serious weakening of your position.

The best time for professional activity is the last ten days of March. During this period, you will be able to solve many problems and to advance steadily.

Money. The financial situation is quite stable. You will have a regular inflow of cash; not always from official sources. It is possible that your business partners will support you. You are likely to conduct successful negotiations regarding loans on favourable terms.

Those who are not involved in business can expect help from family members.

Love and family. Your mind is still fixated on work and consequently you might not have enough time and energy for your family. At the same time, you are a little over-sensitive and do not take kindly to criticism. At the moment everybody needs you and because you are, it seems, irreplaceable, you need to learn how to divide your time between work and play – perhaps you should follow the old advice which says, 'business before pleasure'. If you use your time rationally, you will definitely find the time for fun and this will help you to avoid any grievances both now and in the future. Involving family members in your business could help improve the situation. In other words, if you can find a way to combine the two most important aspects of your life, your loved ones will be grateful to you.

Health. Your energy levels are not high for most of this month. You will have to bear serious stresses and strains, and so it is a good idea to sleep well and to spend your weekends in the countryside if you can.

TAURUS

The first month of spring is marked by meetings, negotiations and discussions of various current problems. Don't rush - let things drift a little.

Business. The problems that started in February will continue into the first ten days of March. Not everything is going according to plan; there are delays in business, meetings are being postponed and promises are being broken. People you expected to support you might sit on the fence and not make any decisions, but this is not a major problem. In the second half of March, everything will fall back into the groove and you will certainly resolve all issues.

Relations with colleagues from other cities and overseas are flourishing. Your plans to start a business in a different city or abroad will be well-implemented. You are likely to have successful meetings and negotiations will be fruitful with good future prospects. Trips that you planned for the second half of the month produce the desired results. The best time for all professional activities is between the 17th and the 30th of March.

Money. One can hardly call the current financial situation stable. It might be that you have to invest in any and all of the possible changes taking place in March. On the other hand, these costs are necessary, and you cannot expect to make any progress without them. That is not a negative for you; all you need do is think and plan several moves ahead.

Love and family. If love is the main thing in your life, you will succeed. After all the possible misunderstandings of the end of February and the beginning of March, everything slots into place. Venus will be present in your birth sign as from the 5th of March and its influence will be stronger after the 10th of March. Thanks to Venus, relationships between family members and lovers will improve notably. Those who are in a relationship with someone from a different city or abroad will be happy. Indeed, in March, you might make the final decision to move to a new place and to start new life with this person. You should try to do everything you can this month as there are difficult times and more adversity ahead.

Single people have an excellent chance to meet a soulmate during a trip or among those who have come from far away. You should grab this chance between the 17th of March and the 30th of March.

Strong couples might begin a move to a new place in a different city or even abroad or just to a different flat or house.

Health. You are healthy, attractive and full of energy this month. Many people who you meet this month will point this out.

GEMINI

You have a wonderful opportunity to show off your negotiating flair in March - you can convince anybody of anything.

Business. The activities you started last month will continue in the first ten days of March, but you might have to revisit the same questions, sort out more paperwork and seek those who can help. You should pay serious attention to the details and leave no stone unturned - this is very important in order not to make any mistakes. You should not sign any important documents, make premature promises or conclude any deals before the 10th of March.

People you meet in the period between the 17th of February and the 10th of March may turn out not to be reliable partners and this will become clear in the course of time. Better times will begin as from the 10th of March and in this period, you will see a protracted stalemate in your business projects finally move forward again with negotiations becoming dynamic and constructive. In short, you will succeed in anything you start.

Money. The financial situation becomes stable in the second half of the month when you can expect both moral and financial support from your partners. There is also a good chance of getting a loan on very favourable terms.

Those who are not involved in business can expect financial help from their spouses or family members.

There is also a possibility of profiting from various real estate activities.

Love and family. Those with family are still busy with various domestic issues and many Gemini will therefore have to resolve both professional and family situations simultaneously. It will not be difficult this time, however, and you will manage to make progress in both directions. Your partner's business is doing well, and you might get something from your partner that improves the family lifestyle.
Young people have every reason to expect help from parents in such important matters as purchasing a flat or house.

Romantic relations become more serious and there is a strong possibility that you will decide to live together.

Women have a good chance of becoming pregnant. However, if you are planning IVF this month, you should not do so between the 17th of February and the 10th of March as there is unlikely to be a positive result during this time.

Health. You could hardly describe your energy levels as stable in March. Periods of activity might coincide with the periods when you lack energy but no matter how busy you are, you should sleep enough. A good night's sleep is the main prerequisite of well-being for almost everyone under this most restless of birth signs.

CANCER

'All that is new is really just something old that has been overlooked' – this sentiment is very appropriate for March and applies, to both work and love.

Business. In the first ten days of March, entrepreneurs and managers will continue to have the same problems that they had in February. All activities take a very long time and there are constant delays. ,Everything will begin to work out better in the second half of the month, however, and you will finally start to see the light at the end of the tunnel. This light becomes brighter each day and eventually you will hit the bull's eye.

Relations with your colleagues from other cities and overseas will become more important and there is a strong possibility of a business trip. If you have been discussing future co-operation with your partners, now is the moment of truth – you will see what you have or have not achieved. Your business partners will play a very important role in all the activities of the month and their influence on your business will be positive.
The best time for all professional events is the last ten days of the month - try to plan all the most important activities for this period.

One more piece of advice – you should be cautious with new people who appear in your life between the 17th of February and the 10th of March for they will turn out to be unreliable and you would be better off not trusting them. –This is true both for work and love.

Money. The financial situation is stable. In March the largest amounts of money might come in on the 6th, 7th, 15th, 16th and the 26th to the 28th.

Love and family. Things are going well in your personal life. Both married couples and lovers will be in harmony with each other this month and will probably plan a romantic trip. ,

Single people might dive into an exciting romantic relationship, but the stars advise that you bear in mind the difficult period from the 17th of February to the 10th of March. You will soon be disappointed by these people if you cannot trust them; those who you meet later will better fulfil your expectations. The stars therefore recommend that you dress up and socialise more in the second half of the month.

Health. In March your energy levels are quite high and there is no need to worry about your health.

LEO

March will be both complicated and contrary. You should not spring into action. The best thing to do now is to look inside yourself and better understand your own needs and goals.

Business. It is a slow season for business. All the activities you planned recently might, for different reasons, get bogged down. In some cases, the right people will not be there to assist but, in other cases you will need to do more work on your projects by correcting mistakes or considering other methods to hurry things along.

During this period, a sensible approach will not only help to achieve your goals but also to boost your profile in the eyes of others. The second half of the month is more dynamic and much more successful, and you will truly be riding high closer to the end of the month.

In the first half of the month clerical workers will be on a losing streak. The stars recommend that you be more attentive to details and try not to make any mistakes at work. It might be a good idea to take a holiday and get some rest from work as you are unlikely to get promoted this month anyway. After the 10th of March the situation will change, and many Leos might expect sudden success.

Money. The financial situation will improve closer to the end of the month, but in the beginning and the middle of March you will have to spend money on your children and/or your partner.

Good money can be expected on the 4th, 5th, the 8th to the 10th, the 17th, 18th, 27th and 28th of March.

Love and family. For many Leos, March is full of family worries. The more time you are able to spend with your kids and relatives, the happier you will feel. Work can wait, especially because the first half of the month is not so positive for professional activities. ,In the second half of March, however, you will be totally absorbed by work and there will unfortunately be no time left for your family.

On the other hand, nobody will stop those in an office affair.

Health. Your energy levels are not high in the first twenty days of March. Those who have chronic problems with their musculoskeletal system, and those who suffer from arthrosis or arthritis should be extra cautious. Young and healthy people are advised to take extra care of their skin and hair, and to visit a specialist if necessary.

VIRGO

*Major challenges can never be solved in the blink of an eye -
you have to spend time and effort on your goals. So, take in
your sails a little and try not to act in haste.*

Business. The first half of the month is tricky. Your relations with partners are still difficult and this causes complications in business activities. On the other hand, now is a good time to discuss, to understand and to solve problems - you may also find the flaws in your projects and be able to eliminate them.
Matters will be clarified in the second half of the month and you will see that all your efforts were not in vain. Your partnership with colleagues from other cities and overseas will be significant and their support will boost your business. Closer to the end of the month, you might have a trip that is quite useful and important.

If you plan to start business in a different city or abroad, or if you are looking for a job far afield, you will be very close to fulfilling your dream.

Money. Progress in your professional activities will improve your financial situation. Many of your birth sign will receive good money at the end of the month whilst others may expect a general improvement in their financial situation. These are not idle dreams but realistic hopes that are to be fulfilled in the near future.

Love and family. In the first half of the month, lovers might, for various reasons, lose contact with each other. It is also possible that you will have to live separately for a time or see each other less frequently due to your hectic work schedules.

A similar situation is possible for married couples, but the situation improves after the 10th of March, and so there is no need to worry about it too much. Your children will make you happy, especially closer to the end of the month. Many families will be blessed with new arrivals - children or grandchildren.

Those who plan IVF should look into the second half of March; this is an ideal time for such treatment. Many of your birth sign will be lucky with natural conception.

Health. Your energy levels are quite high in March and there is no need to worry about your health. The stars advise minimising stress in the first ten days of the month to avoid feeling less energetic and confident.

LIBRA

Your attitude changes with the arrival of March - you are now responsible, organised and efficient.

Business. The first ten days of March are not very dynamic, and so this is a good time to finish up any projects you have started and to sort out other issues, both major and minor.

Managers are likely to undertake a difficult project and employees will not be able to do it without professional guidance. The stars recommend paying close attention to your team. You have brought in some changes lately, but these are not final – there is still a lot to change.

The second half of the month is an ideal time. In this period your business will move forward, expand its territory and win fresh markets.

For clerical workers the second half of March is tense, and you will have a large volume of work. It is unlikely that you will be praised or thanked for this but you ,-nevertheless have every right to be proud of yourself.

Money. The financial situation is generally stable. You will have regular inflows of cash; not always from your main place of work. It is possible to earn additional income from real estate activities. You may also come into inheritance.

Love and family. Many representatives of your birth sign will be torn between work and family and there will be plenty to do at home; you may be busy refurnishing your house, flat, cottage or country house. In the second half of the month, you may realise that the end of these activities is now coming into sight.

Marital relations are balanced. Mutual problems are unifying and will be successfully overcome.

The second half of March is favourable for lovers. Their relationship becomes deeper and they may soon decide to live together.

Women have a good chance of pregnancy in the second half of March.

Health. Your energy levels are not high in March - you need to live a healthy lifestyle. You need a balanced diet and good quality sleep to avoid any future problems with your health.

SCORPIO

Charisma and wit are your defining characteristics in March.
Such qualities are always beneficial in both work and love.

Business. During the first half of the month, routine work and business will be a burden because the main events will be meetings with friends, candlelight dinners and other pleasant occasions. Even business negotiations during this period will be held in an entertaining or romantic setting.

Many of your birth sign will go on a journey on which you are able to combine business with pleasure, rest and renew useful business relationships.

Your relations with colleagues from other cities and overseas are developing well and this becomes most noticeable in the second half of March. During this period, you become more organised, business-like and practical.

In the second half of the month you can expect many meetings with both old and new colleagues. Your relationships with these colleagues will develop really well and in exactly as you had hoped.

Clerical workers might be offered a new job or new responsibilities in their current place of employment. This might involve travelling a lot or moving to a new location and it is quite possible that family ties will play an important role in these events.

Money. The financial situation is unclear, but your hopes of a profit will come true in the near future. At present, you might expect support from your business partners, relatives or family members.

Love and family. For many Scorpions, the main events in March will take place in either family or romantic relationships.

Your relationships with your relatives are still very important to you as they play a major role in your life, both personally and professionally. You might move to a new place, and it is quite possible that some of your relatives will initiate this.

For others, it will be the voice of love that calls from afar. You might renew romantic relations with a former partner who will welcome you with open arms. Single people might meet somebody interesting in the second half of the month. The stars give the green light to all new romantic relationships.

Health. In March your energy levels are quite high and there is no need for you to worry about your health.

SAGITTARIUS

You should spend most of March taking care of your family.
Bear in mind the old saying that, 'my home is my castle'.

Business. As the first ten days of March are slow and unproductive, many of your birth sign will take a holiday or be busy sorting out family problems.

Those at work will have to improve the projects they have started, carry out organisational tasks and resolve outstanding questions. The second half of the month is more productive and successful, and you might receive some new and interesting offers that have good financial prospects. During this period entrepreneurs and managers might employ new people. Clerical workers will either get a job offer or will be promoted at their current workplace.

Money. You are not going to have any problems with money during such a remarkable period of professional development as it brings with it a long period of financial stability. You might expect sizeable income on the 1st, the 8th to the 10th, the 17th, the 18th and the 27th to the 29th of March. There is also a good possibility of receiving bonuses, prizes and presents. Love and family.

Feelings and relationships might be very important this month, especially in the first half of March. By relying on their wisdom and love, many families will continue improving their homes.

You are likely to have friends and relatives visit you in your home more often than usual. Some of your birth sign will become nostalgic and try to find people they haven't seen for a long time in order to renew old friendships.

Lovers will have harmonious relations, especially those with similar professional interests. In the second half of the month, you might fall into an office romance that could develop well in the future. Children make you happy; this is a positive period in their lives, and it is most likely that you will support them in word and in deed, and of course materially.

Health. Your energy levels are low in the first ten days of the month, and many of your birth sign are likely to suffer from an energy deficit and apathy. The last twenty days of March are more dynamic and you will gradually get back into your usual shape and be ready to put some pep and vim back into everyone's step.

CAPRICORN

In March you will find answers to some important questions - both personal and professional - that have been bothering you for some time.

Business. The first ten days of March are not very auspicious. You might face delays and people who might have helped you will have disappeared from the scene. Entrepreneurs and managers of various levels will have to return to the same old matters, finalize documents and doublecheck any mistakes in paperwork. Most of these problems are connected with colleagues from other cities and overseas but this is not a huge problem, however, as you are persistent and determined and everything will be sorted out by the second half of the month. ,

The second half of the month is more successful, and it is a good time for negotiations and business trips both near and far. Moreover, you have excellent chances to succeed with any project and to establish useful business partnerships. If you want to change something in your business or find a new job, there is no better time.

Money. Stern Saturn will move into the financial sector of your sign this month and this means that all financial matters need caution and responsibility. It is possible that in the near future your income will go down and your costs will go up. This concerns both your personal and your professional life and both situations entail serious expense.

Love and family. You will continue to have the same personal problems you have had in previous months. During the first ten days of March, your relations with relatives are not quite balanced, but in the second half of March your efforts to improve the situation will be rewarded.

One could envy your romantic relationship. The planets align in such way that you will not be able to resist your feelings: if you are in a strong relationship, it will become even stronger; if you are single, this month brings plenty of chances to change the situation; if you are disappointed with a former relationship, you will see it differently. The forecast is for a more positive second half of the month.

Your children make you happy. They are having a lucky streak in their lives and you will support them both in word and deed.

All the trips you planned for March will be successful, especially if you go in the second half of the month. If you want to travel in the first half of March, it is better to visit familiar places and be careful with your documents.

Health. Your energy levels are quite high in March and there is no need to worry about your health.

AQUARIUS

All those problems you have been trying to solve for some time will be easily resolved this month. It looks like you have reached the necessary level of understanding.

Business. The first ten days of March are important and practical. Entrepreneurs and managers of various levels will be busy solving financial matters and the stars recommend you be more cautious as the possibility of making mistakes is quite high during the first ten days of March. It is wiser to spend this time discussing and analysing the current situation and to then make decisions in the second half of the month. In this way, you will achieve maximum success and profit.

The second half of the month is a very positive and productive period when all your most ambitious plans and wildest dreams might well come true. If you plan to expand your business, you can expect good results and use this period to your advantage.

Those whose business is connected to property, land and construction will be especially successful.

Clerical workers will be able to improve their professional and financial situations and the ideal time for this is in the second half of March.

Money. The financial situation is stable with a good chance of an up-swing. You will have regular cash inflows and not only from your official place of employment. Many of your birth sign will receive income from selling or leasing out property. Those who plan to sell a business can also expect to profit.

Love and family. Those who live with a partner will spend most of March doing domestic work and solving organisational problems. It is possible that you will move to a new house, finish the renovation of your current home or buy new furniture to refurbish your home. It is also possible that you will sell your house or flat at a profit.

Married couples might be going through changes in their relationship. Even such difficult situations as splitting up and division of property might be resolved without conflict or bitterness.

Couples who have had a long romantic relationship might decide to live together and parents or senior members of the family could assist in this matter.

Many families can expect an addition to their family, and this might happen in March.

Health. Your energy levels are not high this month, but if you live a healthy lifestyle you will not have any serious problems with your health. Many Aquarians tend to gain weight easily and so it is worth keeping to a diet, going to the gym more often and remembering that walks in the countryside are also very useful.

pisces

It will be almost impossible to resist your wit and charm.
These better aspects of your personality will be fully dis-
played in the second half of the month.

Business. The first half of March continues the trends of the previous month. Business matters will still take a long time to solve and important negotiations will drag on for different reasons. The situation is unlikely to change and that is why it would be wise to remember the old saying, 'slow and steady wins the race', which is very apt for this period. –
After the 10th of March, the situation will start to change, and you see that matters start to move in the right direction.

Your relations with colleagues from other cities and abroad develop well. In the second half of the month, you will be able to come to agreement on many matters and this co-operation will be mutually beneficial. All of your initiatives are still under the guidance of your old friends or people of high social standing and their support is essential for the development and expansion of your business, both now and in the future.

Trips that you planned for the second half of March will be successful. If you plan to start a business in a different city or abroad, you will not be able to find a better time.

At the same time, looking six months ahead, the stars advise entrepreneurs and managers to be cautious about signing documents and to scrutinize every legal angle, especially in the case of partnership with colleagues from a different country.

Money. The financial situation is stable. It seems like you already work with wealthy people or perhaps you are about to go to work for a wealthy and profitable company. In both cases, everything goes well!

Love and family. For those who have just started a romantic relationship, your affair will continue successfully. If you are still single you may have a good chance of meeting a new love and this is likely to happen during a trip or among friends who have come from far away. Another possibility is that old friends fix you up with someone!

Those with family will get in touch with relatives living abroad and might even visit them. It is possible that this trip leads to bigger changes in the near future, such as moving abroad.

Health. Your energy levels are quite high this month and there is no need to worry about your health.

ARIES

Your attempts to continue living on your reflexes are likely to lead you up a blind alley. At the moment, you are a person of gravitas, but you should not use your influence unduly.

Business. April is quite a difficult month and the main problem will be in relations with some of your friends or with some high-level officials. As is so often the case, money or financial issues will be the main problem and you are likely to come off worse this time. The first half of the month is the most complicated, especially between the 7th and the 10th of April.

Your relationships with colleagues from other cities and overseas will also demand extra attention. You are unlikely to have any serious problems in April itself, but the following month will show that not everything has been going as smoothly as you thought in this area. This is why you should be more careful and precise in the negotiations now and make sure to sign all the necessary documents in good time.

Money. You can expect heavy expenditure and the possibility of financial losses in the first twenty days of April. The last ten days of the month are more favorable, however. Large amounts of money will be received in the period from the 23rd to the 25th of April.

Love and family. You are going to be facing some tough times in your personal life, too. You are irritable, aggressive and intolerant and this unsurprisingly leads to numerous conflicts with family members. Try to quell your anger and dampen your emotional outbursts in the period from the

6th to the 11th of April as the possibility of a major conflict is highest here.

Parents are likely to also have problems with children in this period and it might lead to sizable costs as a result.

Your relations with kin are quite harmonious, although the near future will show you that the situation is not entirely stable.

Trips planned for April will be successful, especially if they are not between the 6th of April and the 11th - there is a good possibility not only of conflict, but also of injury in these 5 days.

Health. Your energy levels are quite high in April and there is no particular need to worry about your health. If you follow the advice of the stars and use your energy only for peaceful purposes, your life will be easier and more tranquil.

TAURUS

If you have already prepared a list of goals for this month, you may as well rip it up - events are very likely to simply overtake you.

Business. You should exercise caution in April because it will be a complicated month.

Your relations with colleagues from other cities and overseas will become fraught, and a series of problems can be expected in the period from the 6th to the 22nd of April. You may have to overcome some legal obstacles, or you might need to resolve problems with paperwork and contracts. Looking ahead, we can say that although there will be no irreparable damage, your business will lose momentum, and this is not what you need at the moment. Any current problems might worsen in the second half of the year. Clerical workers should be more attentive to their professional responsibilities because there is a good chance of trouble with their management. It is also possible that your company will undergo a reorganization and that you will need to think of other ways to use your talents and abilities. If all of this does come to pass, you should not worry because the old saying, 'whatever happens, happens for the best' is very apt for this period in your life.

Money. Despite all of your professional troubles, you will not have any money problems. You will have regular cash inflows and the approximate dates when larger amounts come in are the 7th, 15–17th, 26th, 27th of April.

Love and family. Your personal life is not all plain sailing either. If you plan to move a great distance, you will face obstacles that have to be overcome before May.

You might have an argument with your relatives, but it is more likely that it will be with your in-laws. You should remember that you are very vulnerable this month and so you need to be cautious and show tact. If your partner or loved one seems detached, you just have to accept this - time will pass and things will fall into place again.

Health. Those who luckily escape personal and professional problems might have some health problems. Your energy levels are not high this month - you might frequently feel tired, lethargic or even depressed. Keep your chin up! All your troubles will vanish after your birthday. You need to take care of yourself and keep everything within sensible limits. You should also be careful while driving and traveling – the chances of injury are high from the 6th to the 23rd of April.

GEMINI

There are likely to be serious changes in April - at work, in your relationship and even in your ways of thinking and acting. It will not necessarily be pleasant, but you need to pull yourself together and brace yourself for both attack and defence.

Business. You will be faced with a number of problems this month. Legal difficulties and an unexpected conflict with colleagues from other cities and overseas are possible in the period from the 6th to the 24th of April.

During this period, you might also have misunderstandings with friends and high-level officials. It is likely that these problems relate to finances and material assets. There will be a spike in such problems between the 6th and the 24th of April. There is a glimmer of hope that the problems can be successfully resolved in May. If the problems do begin to drag on, however, the outcome will be poor - remember this and try to sort everything out this month if you can.

You will achieve more in April if you don't delegate but roll up your sleeves and get down to it yourself. You are the one to succeed!

Money. The financial situation is not really stable in April. Money will run through your fingers like water. This may be related to work or to your personal life.

Love and family. Your personal life in April is quite difficult. Gemini with families will have problems with children and related costs.

For lovers, this month is also quite difficult. You will have a series of disagreements and reconciliations and the stars suggest that your role is that of the peacemaker; you are the one who tries to snuff out all the quarrels and your resourcefulness and imagination will be the key. Keep track of events - this is the only path to peace and love at the moment.

If you have problems with your in-laws, you will again be the one to sort everything out.

You might expect some secrets to come out in the period from the 6th to the 12th of April, causing unexpected complications to family relations. You need to study all the possible options and outcomes carefully beforehand in order to eliminate the root of the problem. As they say, 'forewarned is forearmed'.

Health. Your energy levels are quite high in April, although the stressful situations of this month might mean that you feel tired or exhausted closer to the end of the month. To avoid this, you should sleep more and hustle less. It's hard to see now but all aspects of your life – including your health - will benefit from such a stressful month further down the line.
You should be careful while driving and travelling in the period from the 6th to the 15th of April as there a chance of accident or incident.

CANCER

April is like being in your own thriller – full of tension, shady backroom deals and constant conflict. Emotions run high and this is true for both work and for love.

Business. There are plenty of unexpected changes in the professional sphere. It is possible that you will have serious disagreements with business partners who see the development of the business differently from you. Furthermore, there are likely to be unexpected financial problems not only with your partners but with other key people.

You should be cautious because your partner's position is stronger and if you fall out with them you might be shooting yourself in the foot. You need to be more reserved and tactful; no matter how hard it might seem at times. You should consider all possibilities and try to steadily unravel the tangle. Looking further forward, we can say that most of the problems will be solved at the end of April and beginning of May.

Money. Money is another aspect of your life where problems are possible in April. You should be extra careful between the 6th of April and the 17th of April when the chances of financial loss are quite high.

During this period, it is possible to be faced with theft and other adverse circumstances related not only to money but to other material assets. Those who work in finance such as brokers, accountants and bank staff should be especially cautious.
If you have any debt you should bear in mind that you might be faced with some very tough demands this month.

Love and family. The situation in your personal life is also complicated. All your hopes for a future spent together do not look so promising now. Do not jump to conclusions! You need time to understand how much you need one another, and April is not the best time for making big decisions.

Emotions run high and any conversations may end up with arguments and outbursts of anger. If you are connected to each other not only romantically and by family, but also professionally, your situation will be more complicated still. If this is true for you, you should not allow yourself to be blown away by emotion but to remain patient and grounded. The problems will not last forever and every cloud indeed has a silver lining. At the end of April or the beginning of May, the situation is likely to improve. If it does not, you will find comfort in that you did everything possible.

Health. Your energy levels are not high this month. There is an especially unfavourable period from the 6th of April to the 15th of April when there is a strong possibility of unexpected illness, injury and accident.

LEO

'A veritable obstacle course' - this is how to best describe the main trends this month. However, you are used to it; you have been moving your business forward despite being caught between a rock and a hard place.

Business. Many professionally active Leos will be faced with a number of problems this month. During the first ten days of the month, entrepreneurs will have serious disagreements with their business partners - likely as a result of differing points of view on business development and its financial side. During the second ten days, you might have problems with colleagues from other cities and overseas. The trip you planned might be delayed.

Clerical workers will face competition and there will consequently be an unpleasant situation with management.

Friends or friendly officials are likely to help you out in all the difficult situations of the month. If you need to ask them for help, they will support you in word and in deed. This advice will be of interest especially to those under the pressure of inspection or audit.

Looking further forward, we can say that this month will not bring any insoluble problems and you will see this for yourself by May. So, plan your actions and go ahead accordingly.

Money. The financial situation will improve significantly during the last week of the month and this is closely related to a general improvement in business. Better still, this favourable tendency will continue into May as well.

Love and family. May is very professionally oriented and you might have neither the time nor the inclination for your personal life. For those whose priority is romance and family interests, however, April will not be altogether pleasant. You might be shocked by the aggression of your partner who may be especially vicious in the first half of the month. You will need to be tolerant and non-judgemental and remember that nobody is perfect. This will save you from conflicts and disappointments.

In other cases, somebody in your family might fall ill or go through difficult times - they will need your help, love and support.

Health. Your energy levels are high enough this month, but the stars warn you that April is not only combative but maybe also painful due to the possibility of injury. You need to be cautious while driving and try to avoid dangerous situations.

VIRGO

This month is like a rollercoaster. The good thing about a rollercoaster is that the end is predictable and quite favourable.

Business. Do not expect much from April, and certainly not from the first twenty days. During this period, entrepreneurs and managers might have unexpected problems with colleagues from other cities and overseas due to misunderstandings about work processes or the poor behaviour of your employees. You should investigate all possible variants and take timely and necessary action. By doing this, you can alleviate or even avoid many problems.

During this month you will also face serious financial problems. In any case, you will have many expenses and your costs may even endanger your financial soundness at some points. This is not a true threat - your business is developing, and you will be able to cope with everything eventually.

Clerical workers might have problems with fellow staff due to the un-derhand dealings of your more malevolent colleagues. However, all such unpleasant situations will be compensated for by the support of manage-ment and the high and mighty in your company.

Anyway, you should remember that next month will be better, although there is still a long way to go to reach real success.

Money. April is ruinous. Some of you will have to invest serious money into business development, others will run through major expenses on family needs. You will occasionally receive small amounts of money and this allows you to survive this difficult month.

Love and family. Your relationships with family members will take up most of your time. People with family will be busy solving their children's problems and will spend lots of money on their current needs.

Those who are in love will have a difficult first twenty days of April when the possibility of conflict and misunderstanding is quite high.

The last week of the month is more favourable. Many of your birth sign might have a trip or make plans for a trip. Conflicts will fade away and you will enjoy a more peaceful relationship.

Health. Traditionally, spring is not a good time for health for many of your sign. In this respect, the first twenty days of the month are the most difficult. Only on the 23rd of April, after the new moon, will the situation change, and you begin to feel more energetic - this will improve with each passing day.

LIBRA

Nobody is perfect. You will have to get used to this idea in April. It is also possible that people around you think the same about you.

Business. You will spend most of April settling relationships with your partners and opponents. There is likely to be dispute regarding land and property. Most of the conflicts will happen between the 1st and the 24th of April. After that you will be able to reach a suitable compromise, although it will turn out to be only temporary.

Your relations with colleagues from other cities and overseas look good at first. However, after a month you will realize that the current intentions of your remote colleagues might be changing to some extent. This is why, if possible, you should try to turn any oral agreements into something legally concrete. If you do not succeed, you should be coldly realistic; living under an illusion does not help.

Trips that you planned for April will be successful.

Money. The financial situation in April is not an easy one. Most of your costs are related to children, relatives, renovations and major purchases for your house and family.

If you plan to start a business, you might expend a lot of money on this important and challenging project.

Love and family. You need discipline and control in your personal life. You might have serious disagreements with your partner, who will become aggressive and sharp-tongued all of a sudden. It is possible that you will have to deal with situations regarding a flat, country house or other large property.

Some families will have problems with children and solving them needs money.

Most family related troubles will happen in the period from the 1st to the 24th of April – the difficult situations will cease after that. In all family matters, your partner's relatives will play a very positive role; they will act like peace doves and will help to sort all family disagreements out tactfully.

Pay attention to one more piece of advice - you and your partner should travel somewhere together as this will reduce any tension in your relationship and allow you to talk in a gentler way.

Health. Your energy levels are not high in April. The stars recommend that you solve all your problems with a cool head and not to hustle or stress.

SCORPIO

Do not try to square the circle in April but instead, cover your back. Nobody is without blemish, but those who realise this and eliminate their mistakes, tend to win.

Business. You need to do a large amount of diverse work this month. Those in partnership with colleagues from other cities and overseas will face some sudden problems. There might be issues with organization or a working and balanced system might be affected by legal problems. Entrepreneurs and managers should to pay attention to employees who might damage the business by their actions. Clerical workers will be faced with opposition from colleagues.

If you plan to move and start business in a new city or abroad this month, you might face a number of logistical issues and you will spend all of April trying to resolve them.

The most pressing problems have to be solved between the 1st of April and the 24th of April; after that the situation will start to change.

Money. From a financial point of view, this month is neutral. You cannot expect any big gains, but neither will you experience any big losses. It is possible to expect a little inflow of cash on the 3rd, 4th, 12th, 22nd of April.

Love and family. Your personal life does not look particularly quiet or balanced this month. One reason is that you are fixated on your own ideas; not even trying to understand other people's points of view. Another reason is the strange position of your partner - it seems rebellious to the point of mutiny. It might be that the reason for this disagreement is real estate and you have opposing opinions about whether to buy or sell.

Those who move far away will have other problems, such as the complicated process of preparing the necessary paperwork, legal obstacles or even a breach of the law.

Looking further ahead, we can say that the majority of these problems will be solved at the end of April or in May. These periods are also good for sorting out any situations with your relatives.

Health. April is a very hectic and busy month and you might feel not very confident and energetic as a result. The stars recommend keeping a wise distance from all of the difficult situations this month and remember the words of the King Solomon, 'this too shall pass'.

Drivers should be careful in the period from the 1st to the 25th of April as there is a good chance of unpleasant scenes and accidents.

SAGITTARIUS

You will be busy sorting out a number of problems this month. Although you will get no acknowledgement, credit or gratitude for finding the right solutions, you still have every right to be proud of yourself.

Business. The first ten days of April will bring unexpected problems with colleagues from other cities or overseas. It might happen because of professional misunderstandings or legislative issues. In both cases, it is worth asking for help from trusted partners or a close family member. With mutual efforts, you will be able to find a solution.

The stars suggest that entrepreneurs and managers of different levels should be more attentive to their employees. Some of your staff might be so irresponsible as to think it acceptable to act according to the old saying, 'my way or the highway'. Such an attitude will certainly have a negative effect on your relationship with your partners and maybe on the business itself.

You should be extra cautious when planning your trips for the first half of the month; there is a strong possibility of complications during this period.

Money. The financial situation does not look stable in the first twenty days of April. You will consistently suffer serious expense - mainly related to your children, others close to you and renovation procedures.

Love and family. There are many changes in your personal life. Those with family will focus heavily on their children's problems and spend the lion's share of family budget trying to sort out those situations. It is possible that you will spend large amounts of money on finishing and furnishing your own home or the accommodation of younger family members.

Relations between married couples are balanced, although other family ties are likely to sour this month. You might have an unexpected conflict during the first ten days of the month when spouses perceive their mutual commitments in their own way.

This month is quite complicated for lovers due to possible financial misunderstandings or to differing morals and ethics; it is hard to say which reason is worse. In this situation you should remember that different people have different views on life, and it is only wise to admit it.

Health. You are in good health and full of energy. The stars recommend you be more careful while travelling and driving; in this sense, the most dangerous time is the first half of April.

CAPRICORN

Emotions and relationships will be far more important to you than work, money and career. There is nothing wrong with that; the laundry can wait.

Business. Incurable workaholics will achieve a lot of useful things for their business this month. For example, they will put everything on their desk, in the office and in all current matters in order.

The astrologer believes that you have been working really well recently and so there is no need for you to keep such a close eye on the professional situation at the moment. Entrepreneurs and managers have put together an excellent team on whom they can rely in difficult times. Clerical workers have gained the respect of colleagues by their excellent work. All in all, there is no need to worry about business this month.

Money. You are unlikely to have any financial problems. You will receive enough cash regularly this month and there will be few expenses; your costs will be mainly related to the needs of children and relatives.

Love and family. While your professional life is in order, your personal life will be the main source of negative emotions. It is likely that you are not satisfied with the current situation and you will make your point explicitly to your partner.

It is possible that you will come to a decision that means splitting up with your lover or partner.

In another case, you might have to make a choice between your family and love this month. You must understand that hardly anyone manages to keep a foot in both camps and so you will have to choose what is more important to you – your old relationships or what your new lover might have to offer you.

Many families might have problems with children who are becoming too independent, disobedient or even aggressive. In some cases, a significant part of your family budget will be spent on the needs of your children.

Health. Your energy levels are not high this month and indeed the stressful situations in April might cause problems with your health. It is well known that many illnesses are psychosomatic in nature.

If this is true for you, it would be better for you to follow the advice of the stars and sleep more, do some sport and take long walks in the countryside. The main thing in life is our health; the rest will follow.

AQUARIUS

You should be extra careful to details - fastidious and metic-

ulous. Only this way will you be able to achieve your goals and avoid silly mistakes this month.

Business. The first twenty days of April will be a worrying and not very pleasant period. Entrepreneurs and managers should prepare for various inspections that come like a bolt out of the blue and cause any number of problems.

In a different scenario, you might face unexpected problems with colleagues from other cities or overseas; some of which might be of a legislative nature. Many of your birth sign might have to sort out difficult property situations, or correct documents and past mistakes. You should be prepared for some problems that you have ignored in the past to suddenly crop up and bite you this month. It is also possible that some information, which you would prefer to keep secret, will leak. You should take this information into account, check the weaker points of your work and take any necessary measures. As they say, 'forewarned is forearmed'.

The last week of April is quiet and stable. All of the problems from the first half of the month are now being sorted out one way or another. This positive process will continue into May.

Money. This month is more or less neutral financially. You should not expect big expenses, but neither will you earn a great deal. Only during the last week of the month can you expect income from successful property deals or from a loan on very favourable terms.

Love and family. Many Aquarians will have very important events in their personal life. Many families might be faced with a difficult situation regarding property and it is possible that you will have conflicts with relatives. If you plan to sell, buy, or rent your property, April is not the best time for this. You should postpone your decision until the last week of April or the first half of May - this should allow you to eliminate any mistakes and misunderstandings.

Your children not only make you happy, they might become a real source of support in all of this month's troubles.

Relations between lovers are harmonious; your partner is calm, tactful and ready to help you.

Health. Your energy levels are quite high this month. The stars recommend you be more cautious whilst travelling and driving as the chances of accidents and unpleasant events are quite high in the first twenty days of April.

pisces

April is quite difficult, although generally very dynamic. Do not take big risks and think over all of your decisions and actions carefully. You should understand that no one can always escape the jaws of defeat.

Business. You will be very energetic this month and surely able to get through a lot. However, the only problem is that you might not always be happy with the result. It may be related to finances where you have to spend a lot more than you had planned. You may be disappointed with the attitude of those – either old friends or officials - upon whom you have previously relied.

Entrepreneurs and managers of various levels should prepare for inspections and unexpected problems of a legal nature.

You might face some unintended complications with colleagues from other cities or overseas and this might also be related to a breach of legislation.

The most difficult period will be the first twenty days of April, when all of these situations might occur. The last week of the month will be more positive and May will also be relatively good.

Money. April is unstable in financial terms. Those in business will have to invest large amounts of money in the development of their business. Others might incur serious costs in their personal and family life.

One more piece of advice – do not lend any money this month, even to your closest friends. You might end up in the unfortunate situation of having neither money nor friends.

Love and family. Your personal life is very different. Married couples might be busy setting up home. Even if it is quite hectic, these activities might be enjoyable for people with family.

During the first ten days of the month, many of your birth sign will have problems with relatives. It is difficult to forecast the exact reason for yet another misunderstanding, but there is definitely a reason for concern. That is why you need to consider all possible variants and outcomes in advance and take any necessary steps.

For lovers, this month is not easy due to financial problems and self-interest. As long as you are not mean and do not make mercenary demands on your partner, it should be fine.

Something you have wanted to keep secret might also come to light unexpectedly during this unfavourable period. Remember the saying that, 'those who live in glass houses should not cast the first stone' – it is better to make amends for your sins than to try to hide them.

Health. Your energy levels are not very high this month, so you should live a healthy lifestyle and keep within your limits. Also, the first ten days of April might be dangerous in terms of injury - you need to be very careful during trips and while driving because the possibility of accidents is quite high.

ARIES

Financial matters will have you in a vice-like grip this month,
but there is a well-deserved reward in the end!

Business. In general, this month will be good for professional activity. Your authority and influence are growing, and so all your endeavours and undertakings will really develop in the right direction.

The only negative this month is that after the 13th of May, your colleagues from other cities and overseas will behave somewhat strangely. You will not face vehement hostility; it is more likely that you experience deceit and duplicity. The stars recommend taking this into consideration in advance. If you plan on co-operation, you need to sign any paperwork that could protect you from possible adverse situations. If you cannot, try to be more careful and cautious – check and double-check everything that you are told and promised. It is quite possible that information you are given bears no relation to reality. These recommendations are true between the 13th of May and the 25th of June.

Money. Financially this month is not bad. You will have regular money inflows and the amount will keep increasing. The approximate dates of substantial cash inflows in May are likely to be 2nd–4th, 10th –12th, 20th –22nd, 29th -31st.

Clerical workers might expect some additional income and a pay rise. If you want to move up the next step of the social and financial ladder, you need to address your management with the appropriate proposition. You will be heard and understood correctly. The best time for this will be from the 3rd to the 12th of May.

Love and family. There are unlikely to be any changes in your personal life; probably because the main thing for your birth sign in May will be work. However, many families will have problems with relatives who exhibit strange and cryptic behaviours. They might find out something about you or you might discover some of their secrets. In either case, you need to be diplomatic in what you say because your words might be misunderstood.

In this respect the period from the 13th of May to the 25th of June will be the most difficult. You are unlikely to have any open showdowns, but intrigues behind closed doors are quite possible.

This period is not easy for lovers. It is possible that people around you will spread rumours about you. The best reaction to this will be controlling yourself rather than getting involved in conflicts.

You should be cautious of new people who come your way between the 13th of May and the 25th of June. It is likely that they will not come up to your expectations and will just disappear over the horizon, leaving nothing but a bad taste in your mouth. This is true not only for personal but also for business relationships. On the other hand, this period is good for renewing old relationships.

Health. This month your energy levels are quite high and there is no need to worry about your health. Still, you need to be more careful during trips and while driving in the period from the 13th of May to the 25th of June.

TAURUS

In May the winds of change might well fill your sails. It is a good time to take a step forward.

Business. This month professionally active Taureans will take another step forward in the realization of their ambitious plans. Relations with colleagues from other cities and overseas are developing well, there is the possibility of successful business trips. Those who either plan to move to a new place or to start a business in a different city or abroad will be best able to promote their business in the period from the 1st to the 13th of May.

During this period clerical workers might change their job for a more ambitious position. Regardless of any outcome, there is a chance that merely holding negotiations will lead to success later. Still, both clerical workers and entrepreneurs should be cautious regarding all financial agreements. You should remember that not all those in your network - mainly friends and patrons - are entirely honest.

In this respect, the situation might change for the worse after the 13th of May and become yet more complicated in June.

Money. In May, the financial situation is quite contradictory. On the one hand, you are unlikely to experience a lack of money. On the other hand, you might face financial demands from people who have no claim on your finances. This situation will be difficult to sort out, not least in the period from the 13th of May to the 25th of June. The possibility of a mutually acceptable compromise will appear only after a period of complicated financial activity.

Love and family. Those who plan to move far away will have a chance to test the water first. They are likely to travel, to choose the location of their future home and to take other preparatory steps.

For those who are in love the first half of May will be a good time. During this period, relationships are harmonious and even financial disagreements do not spoil the peace, love and harmony. However, in the second half of the month, financial problems might become a serious issue and the situation will only deteriorate and become deadlocked if you do not discuss everything openly and honestly. You should remember that it is not good to stay quiet about important things. This is exactly the case here.

Health. This month your energy levels are quite high and there is no need to worry about your health.

GEMINI

Slow down a little! In May you should not go leaping into action, especially at work. In your personal life, you should show your best side.

Business. Most of May is not good for activity. The best you can do is put your affairs in order and to finish things you have been putting off. The first ten days will be good for having some rest. Clerical workers or confident entrepreneurs might use this time for a vacation.

It is better for all professionally active Gemini to stay at work in the second half of the month. During this period, entrepreneurs might have some serious problems with high-level officials. It will take not only May but most of June to resolve them.

Clerical workers might have serious problems with managers who turn out to be inadequate or incompetent. During this difficult period, you should not be forceful or aggressive. The stars suggest using the main weapon of your birth sign – adroit diplomacy.

The situation might seem better for those involved in the construction business or business related to real estate. Despite all the current problems, they will be able to earn good money and to move their business forward.

Money. The financial situation looks quite stable in May, but this is not only about your earnings at work. There might be real estate activities, and there is also the suggestion of a loan or financial support from your business partners.

People not in business might expect support from family members and friends.

Love and family. May is an excellent time for putting things in order at home and in your family. Many of your birth sign will enthusiastically continue setting up their home. If some of you have not yet bought a flat or a house, you might decide to do it in the first half of May.

During this period, relations in most families are harmonious and peaceful, although you are likely to have conflicts with your and your partner's parents in the second half of the month.

The second half of the month is not good for many lovers. They are likely to expect a crack in their relationship that will grow and become a serious problem in June. During this complicated period, you should try to make less fuss and not to stress. Try to be more diplomatic, but at the same time do not simply roll over; this might be misunderstood and taken as weakness.

May is good for rest. So, take your mind off business and spend a week or two at the seaside.

Health. This month your energy levels are not high. You need to live a healthy lifestyle and take care of yourself. If you cannot go on holiday, you should have a good massage and take regular walks in a nearby park.

CANCER

It is unlikely that you will be alone this month. At the moment you are in-demand and extremely popular among your acquaintances, friends and partners.

Business. The first half of May is really successful period for meetings, negotiations and discussions of future plans. Even while on holiday, you will continue running your business in an 'online' way. Friends and patrons will be well-disposed towards you and will help you in any way they can. The trips you planned for this period will be successful.

The second half of May is more complicated. Entrepreneurs and managers of different levels should prepare for inspections that will more than likely drag on and cause a number of problems.

In a different scenario, relationships with colleagues from other cities and overseas will get more complicated. Long-distance business partners might act rudely; their actions could harm any budding co-operation.

Furthermore, entrepreneurs and clerical workers should be aware that any ugly errors in their work might be revealed closer to the end of the month.

Money. The financial situation is not quite stable this month. There will be lots of expenses while your income will be low. You might even have empty pockets at the end of the month. The stars recommend being more careful with money, and especially in the second half of the month. This period is not a good one for spending or investing money.

Love and family. The first half of May is good for resting and spending time with friends and like-minded people. Do not be shy in expressing your love for your close friends and family members - this will make them happy. During this period, relations between spouses and lovers are harmonious. You might spend time together with your partner on a holiday, having parties, making new friends and high-up contacts.

During the second half of the month the situation will change slightly for the worse as a result of undesirable information, gossip and rumours. This will have an impact on both your personal and professional relationships.

During this period, disagreements with relatives are possible and it is likely that these misunderstandings will happen with your in-laws. In all the difficult situations in this period, you should try to stay calm and sensible, no matter how difficult it might be at times.

Health. Those who fortunately escape any personal and professional troubles might unfortunately have problems with their health. Remember that the period from the 14th to the 31st of May is not lucky. It is possible that you will have new problems with your health or a recurrence of an old disease.

Drivers should be extra cautious.

LEO

A powerful burst of energy will help you to do and to succeed in many things. The stars advise you to move forward but not to forget to cover your back.

Business. The first half of the month is the best time for all professional activities so try to make the best of this time. Managers will be able to get through to employees, and employees will gain respect from their managers.

The second half of the month is generally favourable, but your relationships with some people become an obstacle to success. The problems may be either with your friends or peers, or with your partners or high-level officials.

In both cases the main reason for disagreement will be money or other material assets.

This situation will develop gradually and it is unlikely that all issues will be raised directly and honestly. You should not cheat yourself. In the end, the main reasons for the current problems will become clear – most likely at the end of May or in June.

On the other hand, it is possible that a lot is at stake and you should not tighten the purse strings.

Money. The financial situation is quite contrary. You might have regular inflows of cash and approximate dates for the arrival of big sums will be 3, 4, 10-12, 20–22, 30, 31. On the other hand, you will also have a lot of expenses; some will be related to business, others to your personal life.

The stars advise you not to lend money - even to close friends - in May and in June. Otherwise, you will be left with no friends and no money.

Love and family. If the situation at work can be considered as positive, your personal life is complicated. It is possible that your partner is annoyed or unhappy about something. It is not so obvious at the beginning of the month, but closer to the end of the month, the problem will come fully into play.

It may concern differing outlooks on life, or finances and the material situation might be the problem. It is unlikely that the situation will improve in May, and it might become still worse in June.

If you do not absolutely insist on getting your own way, the problem might work out all right.

Health. During this month your energy levels are quite high, except for possible stress and emotional difficulties in the second half of the month.

VIRGO

In May, your ideas might be distinguished by their novelty and originality. Even better, many of your ideas will turn out to be both interesting and successful.

Business. The first half of May will be positive and quite successful. During this period your relations with colleagues from other cities and overseas will become important. You might have a successful trip.

Those who stay at home will welcome some visitors from far away and will hold successful negotiations. No matter what the situation in the first half of the month is like, you should remember that to achieve your goals you need to move gradually and constantly check your partners' intentions. In the second half of the month, it will become obvious that their intentions do not look that clear. It might turn out that your colleagues' goals are substantially different, and this will cause inevitable confusion and dithering. Later on, in about two or three months you will face financial disagreements. You should remember this in case of having to sign contracts and other important agreements.

Clerical workers will find themselves in the middle of regular changes at work, with deals possibly going on behind your back. However, you should know that, in the end, nothing really serious is happening. Your position at work is quite stable, so just keep doing your work without any stress or flashes of temper. In no situation should you speak straight from your heart.

Money. Despite a number of professional problems, you will not have any financial difficulties. While it is true that there will not be any big gains, neither will there be any big losses. Everything will go according to plan or perhaps even a bit better.

Love and family. Your optimism and willingness to help make you popular, respected and everybody's favourite in the first half of the month. Lovers and spouses will spend time together during a trip and the new places and emotions will breathe life in their relationship.

Single people and people disappointed by a previous relationship might expect a romantic affair. It is likely to happen during a trip or with people from afar.

During the second half of the month, married couples will face some misunderstandings. This time the problem will be their different attitudes to life and the events that take place. If couples have mutual professional interests, the situation will only become worse. A similar situation will happen to many lovers.

Health. This month your energy levels are high enough and there is no need to worry about any problems with your health.

LIBRA

For most of May, you will be tired of routine and long to run far away and have some rest. Do it! The stars are on your side.

Business. During the first ten days of the month, many Librans will forget about work and will focus on time spent with their loved ones and relatives. Hopeless workaholics will put all business in order and will be able to solve a number of organisational problems.

The first half of the month is good for those involved in the business of construction, real estate, land and property. The second half of May is less successful, however.

If you have partners abroad, you might be subjected to some distasteful behaviour. You will not face open confrontation, but you are likely to face dishonesty and back-stabbing. You have probably known this for some time, but you should be more cautious now as serious conflict and open aggression is brewing.

As usual, managers of all levels should be more watchful of their employees' laziness, incompetence or dishonesty. It is important to remember that a business lives and dies by its staff and act accordingly.

During the second half of the month, entrepreneurs might have an unexpected inspection.

Clerical workers should be more cautious of colleagues and try to avoid making or being the subject of underhand deals. You should also be more careful with paperwork and documents, and listen more rather than talk.

Money. Financially, this month might turn out quite stable. In the first half of the month, you might have additional income from various real estate deals. You may also have help from your spouse, parents or partner.

Love and family. In your personal life, a so-called 'household' period continues. Many of your birth sign will be busy setting up home and the best time for this will be the first half of May. During this period family relations are harmonious. Married couples overcome difficulties with the help of their mutual love, wisdom and patience. Those who haven't yet bought property can use the favourable position of the stars to their benefit.

Those not planning such heroic acts will go to the seaside or just to the countryside house.

During the second half of the month, many families will have problems with relatives; more likely with in-laws.

The second half of the month is also unfavorable for lovers. They are likely to face undesired and disputed information, miscommunication and mutual accusations. During this period you should not stay silent about the problems - no matter how much you want to. You should be straight and share your concerns with your partner. It will be better this way.

Health. This month your energy levels are not high, but you will not have any serious illnesses if you lead a healthy lifestyle. During the second half of May, you should be extra careful while travelling and driving.

SCORPIO

May, and especially the first half, is an excellent time to improve your relationships with many people. This is true both in work and love.

Business. Your energy, vigour and skill in running negotiations makes the first half of May really favourable for your career. Your relationships with colleagues from other cities and overseas will become more active ones and you might have a successful trip. During this period you might sign important deals with big future prospects.

This is a harmonious period and you should reinforce your positions. You should also seal your agreements on paper.

The second part of the month is not that favourable; you might face financial misunderstandings. If you have not taken any measures to financially guarantee your cooperation, you will have to go through protracted and tense discussions.

Money. Financially, the second half of the month is the most complicated time. This is a period of some uncertainty - many financial questions will be up in the air. You will not be able to reach any agreement for perhaps one or two months. Only by July will the situation clear up and the problem be satisfactorily resolved. So, do not omit anything, but pursue your goal gradually - step by step. Any attempt to force the issue might result in failure. This is true for obtaining credit, for your partner's money and for any support expected from your family.

You should also be careful when spending money in the period from the 13th of May to the 25th of June; this is not good time for purchases or investing money.

Love and family. The first half of the month is an ideal time for family and romantic matters. Both married couples and lovers will be able to travel and spend quality time together.

During this period, those who plan to move to a different city or abroad might take the first steps to success. You will spend happy moments with your relatives and friends and you can also expect support in all your endeavours. The situation will worsen in the second half of the month - mostly for lovers when they will be surprised to find out that they have many moral and financial misunderstandings.

Parents might have problems with children in the second half of the month - possibly leading to large expenses related to the needs of the younger generation.

Health. In respect of health, the second half of May does not look positive. During this period try not to stress, avoid any hassles and sleep well. In case of problems, you should remember the words of Solomon from The Book of Wisdom, 'this too shall pass'.

SAGITTARIUS

May is full of tension and work. You may be reminded of an old Soviet slogan, 'everyday work is like a holiday for us'.

Business. The first half of the month is definitely positive for various professional activities. You might get some profit from work you did in the past and you are likely to get new, interesting professional offers. Many of your birth sign might be invited on a very successful business trip.

The second half of May looks less positive and more troublesome. During this period, you might face serious disagreements with your business partners. The main reason is real estate or large property. It is possible that, initially, partners will simply avoid giving definitive answers, although later there will be serious confrontation.

If you plan any serious purchases, you should not do this in the period between the 13th of May and the 25th of June.

In the first half of the month, clerical workers might be offered a new job with excellent financial prospects. Alternatively, they might be given additional tasks and responsibilities that the stars see as having a very positive effect on their future.

Money. From a financial point of view, May is not a bad month. You will have regular cash inflows and there may be a remarkable increase in the amount. The approximate dates in May for the receipt of large amounts are 3, 4, 10–12, 20–22, 29–31.

Love and family. There is a saying, 'Those who are lucky in work are never lucky in love; – this will be quite true for many of your sign in May. Relations with your partner are complicated or, to be more correct, vague. Mutual resentment simmers because both partners are trying to avoid open conflict and straight talk.

It is possible that the heart of the problem lies with real estate issues. Looking further ahead, one might suppose that it will take some time to sort this situation out. So, you need to be patient and not pushy; it will do no good and only cause more serious problems. In the best-case scenario, you might expect improvement from trying to discuss all the questions calmly and openly.

Health. This month you are in good health and full of energy and there is no need to worry about your health. The first half of the month is perfect for working on your fitness, having massages and various spa treatments or having a rest in the countryside. If you have enough time, do not miss the opportunity to do these things. As they say, 'Good health is the main thing, the rest will follow'.

CAPRICORN

May is a month of contrast for you. In the first half of the month, you will be calm, optimistic and confident but the second half will be quite tense and stressful for you.

Business. In the first half of the month, emotions and personal relationships will be much more important to you than your business and career. This does not apply to those in the artistic professions - your creative projects will be at a high tempo and will receive public recognition.

The second half of May is less creative and more stressful. Managers will be faced with odd behaviour from some of their employees who may either be ignoring company rules and regulations or be hatching some devious plot. Later on, inevitably, the truth will out and cause a serious row. In a different scenario, you might have problems with colleagues or employees from other cities or overseas. You should bear this in mind and watch your back.

During the second half of May, clerical workers will face a convoluted plot cooked up by some of their colleagues; this possibly involves rumours, gossip and information that is either plain wrong or falsified. During this difficult period, you should try listening rather than speaking out, and always remember the old saying, 'silence is golden'.

Money. The financial situation is stable, but no more. You can expect neither any serious gains or losses.

Love and family. The best time for romantic relations will be the first half of May. During this period you might have a pleasant trip that will make both strong married couples and lovers happy. The more time you are able to spend with your children and loved ones, the happier you will be. During the second half of the month, many Capricorns will face problems with relatives. If you run a business together, this will make the situation more complicated. If you remember, you had a similar situation last year (2019) but this year it should be less serious and shorter.

The second half of the month will be complicated for people in love. They might have difficulties in communication, a misunderstanding, and as a result of all this, a serious falling out.

In a different scenario, it might be that you are not able to see each other as often as you would like, and this may lead to a cooling of the relationship.

Health. In May your energy levels are quite high and there is no need to worry about your health. In the second half of the month, you should be more cautious while travelling and driving.

AQUARIUS

Most of May will be quiet, creative and even romantic. There is nothing wrong with that - sometimes it is useful to forget about work.

Business. May is not so quiet for those whose business involves land, real estate and construction. They have lucrative contracts and will make a good profit.

Others might spend the first half of May having a rest and being busy with family and household activities.

The second half of the month is not really favourable for business. During this period you are not immune from mistakes and misfortunes. You should not put your skin in the game and make any hasty decisions - this is especially true in financial matters as risks here might incur serious losses.

Money. The first half of the month is quite stable. You might make additional profit from real estate or your business partners. Close friends or relatives might also give you financial support. There is the possibility of coming into an inheritance.

The situation will change drastically in the second half of May. During this period your expenses will grow - in some cases it will be due to business needs, in other cases, it will be related to family needs. People who are involved with finances should be extra prudent as the possibility of losses is high this month.

Love and family. The best place to devote your energy this month is starting to refurnish and renovate your accommodation.

During this period, family relations are harmonious. Strong couples will find solutions to various domestic and household situations. Those who plan to sell or to buy house can do this profitably during the period from the 1st to the 13th of May.

The second half of May will not be very successful. Resentment between lovers over finances, morals and life choices may become conflict and may continue into June.

During the second half of the month parents might have problems with children. A substantial part of the family budget will be spent on solving these problems.

Health. This month your energy levels are quite high and there is no need to worry about your health.

pisces

Time management is the key to success; you should remember not only this, but also the old saying, 'business before pleasure'.

Business. The first half of May is perfect for meetings, establishing new contacts and running negotiations. You will be in great shape and will make an excellent impression on those around you. Your relations with colleagues from other cities and overseas are developing well, and a possible trip will be successful. Even if this trip is mainly for rest, you will still be able to discuss professional matters in a quiet and relaxed atmosphere.

The situation changes after the 13th of May. It becomes important to control everything and everyone even if this inevitably causes problems. You might have misunderstandings with partners who do not readily accept the tough and unbending stance characteristic of many of your sign. The stars recommend you be reserved and try to reach agreement in a peaceful manner - this will help you to avoid many problems both now and next month.

These recommendations are true if some of your close relatives are involved in business.

Money. Financially the situation is quiet and no more than that. You can expect neither big gains or losses.

Love and family. The first half of the month is perfect for social events, having a rest and meeting new people. Single people and those disappointed in former relationships might expect an interesting meeting that could brighten up their lives. For many of your birth sign, relationships with relatives will become more active, in the first half of the month you are likely to meet relatives that live in different cities or abroad.

The second half of the month will bring problems to married couples - you might have problems related to real estate. The range of problems depends on your relations in the past and your intentions for the future.

Nevertheless, you will not be able to solve this problem completely in May and it might linger until next month. The stars recommend not pressuring your partner and others close to you as the response will likely be reciprocal. However, if you have set your mind on conflict you will not need such advice anyway.

Many families might be faced with the common or garden sparring between generations - when children do not want to and parents cannot.

Health. This month your energy levels are quite high and there is no need to worry about any problems with your health.

ARIES

Don't rush the ramparts and don't be too eager for change.
This is a difficult time, when you need to stop, reflect and do
some tidying up.

Business. Those of your birth sign who are professionally active are going to be faced with a difficult situation that began last month. Relationships with colleagues from other cities and overseas are becoming more complicated and might end in deadlock. Your plans for this month might remain uncertain or be disrupted – indeed, the situation might seem completely insoluble.

Unfortunately, this is the situation at the moment. By fall, you will have to have solved many problems that are to happen during the summer. However, you will do your best to find the solution and finally you will.

In a different scenario, you might have complications with inspection authorities that last for most of the summer.

Entrepreneurs and managers are recommended to be attentive to their employees. As for clerical workers, they should be cautious of their colleagues. Toxic relationships and clandestine deals among staff members will have their impact on the working process.

It is also possible that some of your opponents will try to bring to light something you have been trying to keep secret - you need to be cautious and cover your back.

Money. With such a complicated possible situation at work, problems with money are also possible. You are unlikely to see big losses although expected profits might not arrive and costs will exceed income. Your past earnings will allow you to weather this situation.

Love and family. Those who manage to escape professional misfortunes will be faced with challenges in their personal lives. Many families will go through complications with relatives, who either behave disgracefully or find themselves in a difficult situation.

In any case there will be plenty to worry about and the stars recommend not following your emotions - no matter how strongly you feel - but sorting all the problems out sensibly. It is possible that this is not the first time you have had to deal with such situations, and so you might have a better idea of how to cope with such tough times.

You might have various problems with property that will probably last all summer.

Health. Your energy levels are not high in June, but this is not really surprising given the difficult emotional atmosphere this month. You need to be more careful with your health and if you cannot cope with your emotions, at least try to sleep well.

You should also be cautious while travelling and driving as the possibility of accidents and unpleasant situations on the road is quite high in June.

TAURUS

Material assets might be of a high priority to you this month.
You will have to balance your abilities with your ambitious
plans and the circumstances in which you find yourself.

Business. For professionally active Taureans, June will be quite a tough time. The main problems this month might be relationships with friends, co-workers or high-level officials. Money or other material concerns might still be the main reason for possible misunderstandings – the resultant conflicts will last not only throughout June but also for the most part of July.

Furthermore, from the middle of June, you might face difficulties with paperwork and documents that could also last for quite a period of time – not less than six weeks to two months.

Those planning to move or start a business in a new place or abroad might face the same problems; they will have to overcome various legal obstacles.

Those who do not move might be faced with inspection by the authorities or some legal problems and it would be wise to prepare for such situations beforehand.

Money. The financial situation looks really unstable – taking into account the problems in the professional sphere, this is not a surprise.

Those whose job is related to finance – bankers, brokers and accountants, for example – should be extra cautious. Others of your birth sign are recommended to protect their property, not to lend any money and not to promise anything to anybody as it will be quite difficult to keep these promises in future.

Love and family. Those who are in a relationship will have to face difficulties. Lovers might have regular conflicts; the main reason for possible disagreements might be differing views on life, divergent personal values or, worse, financial difficulties. There is nothing good about feelings and money being dependent on each other and it is worse still when both parties pursue only their own personal aims. The feelings of many couples will be severely tested this summer; possibly to the point of destruction. This is sometimes useful in life as it is always good to know one another better before a long journey together; the upcoming tests will clearly reveal your partner's true nature.

Many families will have problems with relatives but it will be possible to resolve them in the end.

Health. Your energy levels are not high in June due to the stressful and chaotic atmosphere of this month.

If, by some quirk of fate, you find yourself in a difficult situation, you should remember that sleeping well and having regular strolls outdoors are very important. Summer will be summer!

GEMINI

Again, life is full of struggles and changes! Again, life is in full swing but it might be a bit of a challenge at times!

Business. Your professional life will be exciting and hectic and to some extent unpredictable this month.

Clerical workers will face some changes happening within the company. It may happen because of changes in management or because of changes in the focus of company operations. In both cases there are likely to be certain problems with management. In the worst-case scenario, this might mean dismissal or resignation, but with possible compensation or back-dated wages. This situation might last quite a long time, but looking further forward we can expect that you will get your own back, although not quite as you expect.

Entrepreneurs can continue the reorganisation of their business. This month they might be faced with countermeasures from some institutions or the powers that be. The situation might be quite complicated and require additional resources. However, you should know that you will find a way to change the situation - most likely using a backchannel method.

Money. The financial situation will remain unpredictable for some time. You can expect a little money on the 3rd, 4th, 11-13th of June, although the arrival of more substantial funds will be delayed until the middle of July.

Love and family. Your personal life might take a back seat to your work. For those whom life means love, you might suffer a lack of attention from your partner or unexpected hostility from in-laws. Financial misunderstandings are also possible this month.

Those who happen to be involved in the family business or who work in the same company as each other will have a lot more problems. In this case, professional problems will definitely influence your personal life and it could become a real battlefield. If this happens you need to be clear about what really matters and not make snap decisions. You should remember that it will take time to understand the full picture. As the old saying goes, 'more haste, less speed'.

Health. Although your energy levels are sufficient this month, you need to ration your strength. You should think several moves ahead and remember that the main remedy for your birth sign is sleeping well.

CANCER

This month you will be burdened with a number of problems that seem insoluble at first. As they say, 'a journey of thousand miles begins with a single step' - this so very true for you!

Business. Most of the month is not very lucky. People involved in business will be faced with many misfortunes that might damage their reputation and undermine their positions. There is the possibility of undergoing inspections or the resurfacing of old legal problems.

The behaviour of partners from other cities or overseas might be not exactly friendly or correct and co-operation might go wrong for some time to come. You will need lots of time and an incredible effort to stabilize the situation. So, if you can bear the serious tensions of this month, you will succeed! Don't get yourself down because of possible worrying news - it is unlikely to be completely true and the situation might not, in reality, be that bad.

Clerical workers should take a break from work and deal with family or health matters. There is unlikely to be any progress at work, but problems, conflicts and clandestine deals are quite possible. The stars recommend listening rather than speaking because you might be misunderstood.

Money. The situation with money is quite ambiguous and complicated.

You should try to cut down on your expenses and those of your family members. This situation will last for a few months but you can then expect a more positive period.

Love and family. Problems in your personal life are also possible. You should remember that some unpleasant secrets might be revealed this month that cause complications in the relationships with your partner and in-laws - conflicts are possible for the whole month. During this period, you should remember that you are very vulnerable, and people tend to see your weaknesses rather than your strengths.

Furthermore, being unable to concentrate and not being in the right place at the right time might lead to some cruel and unpleasant jokes being played on you.

To cut a long story short, June is hardly your finest hour and so you need to be more flexible, diplomatic and modest.

Health. Those lucky enough to escape personal and professional misfortune might have problems with health. It is possible that you will come down with the recurrence of an old disease or have new problems with your health. Also, you should be more cautious while travelling and driving as the possibility of accidents and unpleasant events is quite high this month.

The stars recommend cancelling long-distance trips because they will cause nothing but problems.

LEO

For most of June, you will be trying to resolve a difficult situation that has been brewing in your network recently. There are so many players involved that you may feel like giving up. Don't! Don't let it get you down!

Business. In June, you need to realise that all daunting tasks need investment. This might cause serious misunderstandings with friends, co-workers or high-level officials.

On the other hand, it may just simply be the moment when you realise you have to invest in your business. Your expectations of support from others might, unfortunately, turn out to be a false dawn. This is true for entrepreneurs and those who have recently started a business. Others are recommended to be careful with friends and to pay off all outstanding debts.

Lending money is not recommended during the summer months as it could lead to some misfortunes later. Generally, this is a quiet period for business, and this will be especially obvious after the 18th of June. The best you can do in this period is to put your affairs in order, make any necessary amendments to projects and prepare for the more active period that starts as from the end of August and beginning of September.

Money. This month looks quite complicated financially. Your money will constantly ebb away due to both your business and your personal life.

Love and family. Your personal life looks neither smooth nor peaceful. Lovers will have constant conflicts and arguments, and one of these might well be the final one.

You should not get up a head of steam and thus act in haste. It is worth taking a timeout to think things over - to try to understand the underlying nature of your arguments and their inevitable outcome. This might help .you to get out of the crisis with minimum losses and could probably save your relationship.
Parents are likely to have problems with children, along with related costs.

Health. This month your energy levels are not high. You are likely to be on an emotional rollercoaster and so might feel unwell periodically; this will be especially noticeable closer to the end of the month. The stars recommend that you do not worry for no reason. You should remember that stress causes all sorts of illnesses - sleep more and have regular meals.

VIRGO

You are full of energy this month! However, you should be careful to steer it in the right direction and harness it only for good. It will be difficult, but it is possible!

Business. You will be very active professionally this month, but you will not have a quiet life - almost all of June involves conflict with your business partners. Because of this you run the risk of becoming irritable, aggressive and inconsistent in some aspects of your work. The reason for possible disagreements might simply be differing views of business development, or in the worst-case – the possible collapse of the business. At the moment the ball is in your court and although you expect to eventually be on the winning side, you will have to play hard.

Clerical workers will be faced with rivalry and if this is the case, they will have to address their management team directly, from where they will get support and understanding. It may be that the results will be mixed at the beginning, but in the end everything will turn out well.

People in all walks of life should be more cautious of friends or those higher up the food chain. It is unlikely that you will be able to completely rely on them and this will become quite evident in the second half of the month. They might have neither the proper authority nor the will to solve your problems.

Money. This month is quite stable financially. Thus far, turf battles and fights for a place in the sun do not influence your financial situation. Even if some payments are delayed, it will not cause any serious problems.

Love and family. If your personal life is a priority, you should expect some turbulence and change. You might have some serious disagreements with your partner and if you have common professional interests, the situation will be worse.

In a different scenario, either you or your partner might become too preoccupied with various other matters and this will cause quarrels and conflicts.

Your love affair is not developing in quite the way you wished. Your disappointment might be quite serious this month, but in the end, it will turn out to be only temporary. So, you should not jump to conclusions and try to save face.

Couples having issues might be brought back together by their children; their influence on the family situation is definitely positive.

Health. This month your energy levels are quite high. You should not worry much about your health with the exception of the stress caused by emotional distress.

LIBRA

Do not waste your time and effort on the undeserving. You should concentrate on solving your own problems and doing what you think necessary. If you can do this, you will finally be able to get out of the troubles in which you unintentionally find yourself.

Business. The main problem this month is your complicated relationships with colleagues from other cities and overseas. Time and time again you will come up against historical problems that were never completely resolved. You will have to spend a significant amount of time and effort in trying to reach your goal. You will have to be consistent and navigate your goal step by step.

Another problem this month will be your relations with colleagues and employees. Once again, they might damage your business by their incompetence and lack of professionalism. This is not new, but this time you should take the bull by the horns and shore up your position once and for all. It might be a good idea for the managers to get rid of those employees unfit for their positions. Clerical workers should be cautious of colleagues and try not to take part in their clandestine dealings.

You are likely to be fed a lot of falsified, altered or misleading information this month - do not jump to conclusions but act patiently and sensibly.

It is a good idea for entrepreneurs to prepare for any checks, audits or other inspections that might cause many problems this month.

Money. This month is quite neutral financially. The amount of professional problems will not lead to your downfall, but you might well experience an increase in costs and the resulting drop in profits. You should control your financial situation tightly. It is not a good time to make any serious purchases as they might turn out to be both poor quality and unnecessary.

Love and family. Your personal life is also passing through a time of trouble. You might expect to have various problems with real estate or large scale property. You might have to go through tortuous paperwork and red-tape or to fight the authorities tooth and nail for your interests.

Some families will go through misunderstandings with a close family member or relatives. Again, the sticking point will be real estate or other major property problems.

You should be patient because all the problems that have started this month – whether personal or professional - will continue into July.

Health. Your energy levels are not high this month but if you take extra good care of yourself and keep to your limits, you will avoid problems with your health.
Drivers should be cautious as there is a high possibility of misfortunes and accidents this month.

Those who suffer from chronic liver, vascular or orthopaedic problems should be extra careful.

SCORPIO

It may seem that the dice are loaded against you in June but this is not strictly true. You will go through some unexpectedly difficult training this month - this is just tempering the steel that is you.

Business. Professionally active Scorpions are moving forward and there seems no stopping you. This may not be for the best at the moment, however. Slow down a little!

Serious success is next to impossible this month and avoiding problems will be very difficult. If you can have a break and go on holiday, you should do so in order to disengage from work. If this is not possible, do not spring hastily into action but be sensible and cautious when problem solving.

Many Scorpions will have to deal with a lot of organisational work that demands extra responsibility and funds from you.

Those who plan to move to a new place or to work in a different city or abroad might be busy organising this challenging enterprise.

In some situations you might lack support from those around you. However, if you are confident in your decisions, you should evaluate the workload, review your options and prepare for the more responsible stage in your life that starts as from the end of June into August and September.

Money. Financially, this month is quite unstable if not downright destructive. You will constantly haemorrhage money due to work or issues related to your personal life.

Love and family. You will suffer disappointments in your personal life this month. Those in love might unexpectedly find themselves falling out of it. In most situations, the main reason for this mutual discontentment is financial matters. If you can decide that love is more important than money, you may be able to avoid these problems.

Your partner might become demanding and even aggressive; indeed, this might be partly justified by your past promises or present parsimony.

Parents will have problems with children and again they will need money to resolve the situations. Those who are moving far away will have to resolve difficult domestic problems that also require financial outlay.

Health. Those who have happily avoided personal and professional difficulties will have problems with health. Your energy levels are not high in June and this might cause the aggravation of an old disease or the onset of new problems.

You should take care and avoid dangerous situations!

SAGITTARIUS

Diplomacy is not really your strongpoint. At the moment, it is important to remember that there are other equally important points of view apart from your own.

Business. June is a complicated time in the relationship between you and your partners and there may even be occasional outbreaks of trench warfare. There might be disputes concerning large properties. Regardless, you will face the Janus like approach of certain people who will play games with you and try their hardest to worm their way out of things. As a result, your joint business may well suffer.

Looking further ahead, and assuming that your business will be an enduring one, it is not so vital that you are unable to reach a compromise in the short-term. At the moment, therefore, you should concentrate on avoiding silly mistakes and being in too much of a hurry to act. Remember that time is on your side.

Clerical workers will have to put up with criticism, rumour and gossip. This will have a negative impact on your work and your relationship with your management team. If this is the case, you need to be wary and not take sides in any clandestine deals amongst the other staff; this is a good way to fall out with many people and end up being the fall guy.

One more piece of advice for Sagittarians irrespective of their occupation - you should hesitate in taking other people's word for it and only judge people according to what they do rather than what they say. This will save you from disappointment, deceit and other problems.

Money. You should be most careful with your finances and especially with regard to major purchases or sales. Do not rush into things! An old maxim is very true at the moment, 'haste makes waste'. This is true for your financial situation not only in June but also in July.

Love and family. In many cases, the main events of June will take place in your personal life. Strong couples will be busy planning to sell or buy a house or flat but this will turn out to be extremely stressful and complicated. Your partner might have strong opinions regarding current events and so become stubborn and irascible. You are likely to also have some financial disagreements.

Couples in difficulty might start divorce proceedings and the primary issue will be the division of property. According to the stars, there is very unlikely to be a peaceful settlement to this. It is also unlikely that your partner will agree to your conditions, and discussions will become bitter and protracted. Also, questions regarding your children's future might be complex, distressing or even insoluble.

Health. Your energy levels are not high this month and this will become most noticeable closer to the end of the month. Try to sleep well and spend as much time as you can in the outdoors – this should be possible as the weather is usually good.

CAPRICORN

Sometimes in life you cannot do just as you wish; you must do what needs doing. June is exactly like this – you will have to steadfastly weather some new challenges in your life.

Business. The first summer month will turn out to be full of worries and labor. Entrepreneurs and managers should put their house in order in terms of staff and be careful of certain employees who might cause some serious problems to the business by virtue of their actions and underhand deals.

Those who have partners in other cities and overseas will also face some problems. You are the only one able to fix the possibly complicated disagreements related to work. You should take firm control of the situation - only you can cope with it all!

Disputed situations with partners, clandestine deals and instances of doublespeak are also possible; these naturally cause complications on the path to the common goal.

Despite all the possible problems you will have to deal with during this quite complicated month, there is one thing which your partners will have to consider - you alone are handling the situation. Your position is much stronger, and everybody knows this. It is therefore in your power either to ratchet up tensions to breaking point or to de-escalate and smooth the difficulties over - you have a rare freedom of choice and action now.

Money. Despite any professional misfortunes, the financial situation is fine to this point. You will have regular inflows of money without any delays in receipt.

Love and family. Your personal life looks bumpy and unsettled in June. Your relationships with relatives will worsen because of either some mutual commitments or some aged debts. In a different scenario, your relatives will have their own problems that you will have to sort out.

Romantic relationships this month do not develop in the way you may have expected or dreamt. Claims, counterclaims and resentment might become more or less a constant, nagging feature and could thus lead to genuine disillusionment in the relationship.

Relations between married couples are also strained. Most of the problems will be related to joint real estate; there might be problems with renovation and refurnishing. In a different and more complicated case, it might also mean divorce and the division of property.

Health. This month your energy levels are not high and so you need to spoil yourself a little - perhaps with a spa visit or a massage, swimming or just a nature walk. The choice is yours.

Finally, you should be more careful while travelling and driving this month.

AQUARIUS

Do not be over-critical of those around you as it will not help you to avoid conflicts, misunderstandings and other prob-

lems. This advice is true for both work and for love.

Business. It will be quite difficult to focus on all the matters at hand this month. The usual errands might be challenging, all-consuming and still not get finished. You should pay extra attention to financial matters because there are some problems in this area - you might be faced with unexpected costs as a result of general instability or even chaos in your business.

Managers should be attentive to their employees in the second half of the month as they might not behave responsibly or carry out their work competently. During this period clerical workers will face tensions and underhand deals among fellow members of staff. It will be difficult to sort out all the situations, so do not jump to ill-judged conclusions and try to avoid conflict. You should also remember that not everything said is true, and that many decisions taken in June will have to be reconsidered later. All professionally active Aquarians, irrespective of their line of work, should take this into account.

Money. The financial situation is not stable. You will haemorrhage money regularly due either to work or to your personal life.

The astrologer advises you to be extra cautious because Mars, known as an aggressive planet, is in the financial sector at the moment.

Those who are directly involved in finance – accountants, bankers, brokers and so on – should be more than cautious. You cannot expect a profit this month, and financial losses are quite possible.

Love and family. You might face some difficulties in your personal life too. Parents will have to sort out their children's problems and invest a substantial part of the family budget in their education, a holiday or other miscellaneous expenses. The stars recommend that you consider all such expenditure thoroughly because you might well over-spend.

You should also be careful with your other expenses; June is not the best of times for expensive purchases and major investments.

Many loving couples might start or continue to grow apart or perhaps even fall out unexpectedly. This is a difficult time in all respects, so keep your head and do not go shooting from the hip. It is very difficult to determine just who is right and who is wrong at the moment. If something is not right in your relationship, try to explain your concerns tactfully or perhaps just take a break.

Health. You are in good health this month and positively brimming with energy if a bit over-anxious and fidgety. If you do get tired, there should be no problem in having a couple of days break in order to escape the routine and the humdrum.

pisces

This month you will try to sort out a complicated situation but there are so many players and difficulties involved that you will give up in despair...

Business. This month is not favourable for professional activity so it might be a good idea to go on holiday or to start focussing on family problems. Those who stay at work will have to resolve a disputed situation involving certain partners and maybe also some organisational matters that will change the business structure.

In case of the deadlocked situations that are entirely possible in June, you should ask for help from friends or friendly patrons. This will significantly reduce the risk of losses and will help to find agreement with partners bent on opposition. In many cases, the issue will be connected to real estate or large property. Looking further forward, you should know that it is unlikely that all the situations will be completely resolved this month; it is likely to take June and almost all of July to finally sort everything out.

Money. The financial situation is not quite so stable in June; this is unsurprising given the complications in your professional field. Your costs will increase, and your profits will drop - you may do no better than to break even this month.

Love and family. Many of your birth sign will see the main events of June happen in their family and at home. Couples already in distress will have disagreements regarding real estate or property, and many family members will get dragged into this. It is difficult to predict what will happen in each and every case, but there are plenty of reasons for concern. Mars is present in the sign of Pisces and this means that you might become undiplomatic, too direct and even aggressive - any attempt to reason with you will then lead only to further and further escalation. You should try softening your stance because only this might make things better. This is also true for many squabbling couples.

Health. Your energy levels are not high this month. Furthermore, the numerous disputes in your personal life might begin to consume you. You should remember that, generally speaking, no situation is totally insurmountable and that your health is more important. Take better care of yourself. Try sleeping well and living a healthy lifestyle.

ARIES

Do not take risks in matters related to work and finances. The calmer you are this month, the better your surrounding circumstances.

Business. The first half of July is not a good time for important decisions or involvement in any professionally related matters. The best thing that you could do is go on holiday and spend some time with your close friends and relatives. If you cannot do so, you could possibly work on projects which you have started or get on with some organizational work to get your affairs in order.

In the first half of the month, clerical workers should not address their management with any requests, and especially not with any demands. Entrepreneurs and managers should not initiate contact with bureaucracy; if you do happen to have to deal with bureaucrats, try to be cautious and, if possible, play for time.

This is especially true in the case of real estate or problems with plots of land. It will be next to impossible to resolve all of the disputed questions in the summer months, but the situation will change closer to the autumn; things that cannot be sorted out now will be fixed surprisingly quickly then.

Money. Financially, July is not so bad. You will receive reasonable sums of money at the very beginning of the month and then in the middle and at the end of July.

Love and family. This month is not such an easy one in terms of your personal life. Strong couples will face various problems related to real estate, and it is possible that there will be disagreements regarding household arrangements. Unhappy couples may experience conflict over property and housing disputes and devote the whole month to solving the most difficult question: to whom does it belong and in what share.

Relations between lovers are more peaceful and harmonious, but parental interference in your relationship might lead to conflicts which sour the generally tranquil atmosphere of July.

Health. Your energy levels are not high in July, so take care of yourself and pay attention to your diet. The risk of food poisoning is quite high this month.

TAURUS

Try not to reveal your ambitious plans to those around you - rely only on yourself. You don't want anybody to put a spanner in the works!

Business. This month is quite tumultuous for all professional activities. Entrepreneurs and managers should prepare for inspections that could turn out to have undesirable consequences.

Those planning to establish relationships with colleagues from other cities and overseas and to start a business in faraway locations might face difficulties in July. In some cases, issues related to the relevant legislation need to be resolved. In other cases, issues with the law or with the inspection authorities and their requests need to be merely smoothed over.

All Taureans should be suspicious of the information that you receive. Be careful to cover your back as some unpleasant secrets, which could damage your reputation and thus have a negative effect on your future, might emerge this month.

Looking further ahead, we can say that this situation is unlikely to be resolved in July, and the problems are likely to persist until September.

Money. Financially, July is quite neutral. Your costs are balanced by cash income and you are unlikely to go bust. However, the stars advise you not to trust those around you implicitly, especially those offering to assist you. If you are asked to pay or to provide something of material value in return for this help, you are being cheated either directly or indirectly; it is more than likely to be a deceitful or a fraudulent hoax.

Love and family. If your interests lie in your personal life, you will also be faced with difficulties. Many families will have problems with relatives; there may be disagreements, conflicts or other issues with close relatives.

Lovers might find themselves in the center of rumour, gossip and criticism from all sides. If this happens to you, be cautious and prudent and try not to irritate the situation as any conflicts might then snowball. You should also remember that information you receive this month might turn out not to be totally accurate, and so you should be wary of drawing any conclusions from it.

Health. Not only is July a month of conflict, it is also very dangerous in terms of injury. Drivers and those planning trips and should be especially careful as accidents are a possibility for the whole month. The stars recommend cancelling all trips, especially long ones, because there might be some misfortune that causes nothing but trouble.

GEMINI

Try not to make mistakes as they might turn out to be costly ones. The old adage, 'step by step one goes far' will be very true for you this month.

Business. The main problem in July might be money or other material matters that simply leech away all your time. It may be a result of necessary investment in your business or with the excessive activities of your friends or co-workers. Either way the situation requires you to control the people around you - this is a must for your work this month. You should also be careful with paperwork and various other details, especially when dealing with major purchases such as real estate. The stars do not recommend signing important documents in the first half of the month because Mercury, your patron, is moving backwards and the chances of making mistakes are therefore quite high.

The best tactics for this time are to analyse everything carefully and to try to gauge and thus correct any possible mistakes. In other words, you should prepare scrupulously for the more predictable second part of July.

Clerical workers might be faced with unpaid wages and other financial difficulties, but they will be able to resolve these problems towards the end of the month.

Money. July will be quite difficult financially. You will suffer from a constant drain of money due to work or the needs of your family and children. Moreover, it is possible that you will either lose or have money stolen in July.

The stars advise you not to lend money - even to close friends - as otherwise you will end up with neither friends nor money.

Love and family. Important events will take place in your personal life. Many families will decide to buy a house, a flat or a country house or, more modestly, just to buy some new furniture and amenities. In either case, the stars advise you not to make any final decisions in the first half of the month so as to avoid making any stupid mistakes. You should consider all the possible options and only act afterwards.

Lovers will also go through a difficult time. It is possible that they will have to make some serious decisions; even whether to stay together or to take the difficult and painful decision to split up.

In any case you should not rush but consider the situation from a financial point of view; everything might change dramatically in the future.

Health. Your energy levels are not high in July. This will be felt especially by the elderly and those with chronic digestion or musculoskeletal problems. They should take care of themselves and visit a reliable physician if necessary.

CANCER

Buckle up your armour! The possibility of battle is quite high this month!

Business. A very difficult and combative month is ahead of you. Entrepreneurs will be faced with complicated negotiations where the main dispute might be mutual business interests, money or large property. The stars strongly advise you not to rush into things between the 1st and the 14th of July, no matter how much pressure you are under from circumstances and deadlines. Making haste will be your mistake so don't be nervous and flustered but rather consider all the possibilities rationally. In the case of legal problems, you should involve responsible and reliable specialists. You should also remember that your opponents' positions are quite stable and so you are unlikely to solve the problem peacefully. It is possible that you will have to walk many roads and study a lot of paperwork to defend your property.

Those who have relationships with colleagues from other cities and overseas will also face a number of problems. It might be difficult to reach out to your foreign partners, so be patient and try to solve your problems calmly. You should not expect any help with your issues between the 1st and the 15th of July as this time looks very unfavorable. Some problems are likely to be sorted closer to the end of July, others in August.

Money. Financially, the first twenty days of July look unstable and unclear. Only at the end of the month might you expect good money. You should be careful with your money and cut down on your expenses - this will help you to avoid many problems both now and in the future.

Love and family. Those who have long-standing problems in their personal life will undergo another series of property fights where your spouse or long-term partner is very confident and even aggressive. It is possible that you will have to take a serious decision in July – whether to stay together or to part and travel your own path. In many cases the second variant is more probable. If you are engaged in business together, the situation will be worse and you can expect a long battle over the partition of your business. The chances of getting what your want are small and so you should try to compromise and learn to come to agreement with your partner; no matter how hard it might be at times.

Health. Your energy levels are not high this month. Don't forget that a good night's sleep and walks in the countryside are very useful when trying to sort out your feelings and emotions.

LEO

The most difficult month of the year lies ahead for you. You should rely on nobody but yourself and pay great attention to the details!

Business. From a professional point of view this month is, without doubt, an unlucky one. For much of July, you will be tired of your everyday routine and you will long to escape and have some rest. However, you will only manage to do this if all your affairs are in order.

Entrepreneurs and managers should prepare for the inspections and checks that are highly likely to happen at the end of June or the beginning of July. In a different scenario, you are likely to face problems with colleagues from other cities and overseas which delay and complicate your business.

Clerical workers are likely to have some misunderstandings with colleagues, possibly due to stair-well gossip. Delays, protracted tasks and other troubles in your work are also possible.
The first half of the month is complicated in all respects, but the tensions will then begin to ebb away slowly and gradually.

The stars recommend all professionally active Leos to work diligently and not to make haste. You should also keep a very close eye on the details and be careful of them coming back to bite you. Only in this way will you be able to avoid mistakes and achieve your goals.

Money. The financial situation looks quite unstable and the resulting problems will require a lot of money. In some cases, the problems will be related to your work and business or in others to your personal life. Nevertheless, money will keep coming in occasionally and this will help you to survive the month. The approximate dates for the arrival of larger sums in July are the 1st, 2nd, 14th, 15th and the 23rd to the 25th.

Love and family. If your focus is on your personal life, problems are possible here as well. It is likely that some of your close relatives will have misunderstandings at work or health problems, and that you will have to help them out in both word and deed.

In a different scenario, you might feel slighted, unappreciated or that you are not needed. While it's perfectly possible that things truly are this way, you will not be able to address this at the moment. When July is finished, these problems will recede - you just need to be patient and wait it out.

Health. The energy levels of most Leos are quite low this month. Try not to get too emotional about all of July's problems - sleep more and be careful while driving and on trips. The possibility of an accident is high this month!

VIRGO

During July, you will devote much to sorting out difficult situations around you. There are many players and your main priority is to compartmentalize.

Business. The main problem this month might be your relationships with friends, co-workers and some high-ranking officials. It is likely that the main difficulty will be over money or other financial issues and a peaceful settlement to this is unfortunately not possible at the moment.

Your arguments are likely to last until the end of summer or the beginning of the fall, and only then will it be possible to reach a compromise. Another possible problem this month will be delays to your plans and projects caused by a lack of the right people, among other circumstances. It doesn't pay you to begin new long-term projects now; it is unlikely that you will have either the strength or the assets to finish them. However, the time will come - it is right around the corner - and things will work out as you wanted.

Your relationships with colleagues from other cities and overseas might be suspended and only closer to the end of the month will the situation progress.

Money. The financial situation looks ruinous this month and your money simply drains away in all possible directions. In some cases, it will be related to your work or business, in others to your personal life.

Love and family. Things are complicated in your personal life, too. Parents will be concerned about their children's problems and will invest a lot of money in their up-bringing and education.

In July, lovers will be caught up in misunderstandings and arguments as a result of differing outlooks on life, differing values and possibly mutual financial problems. It is not a good thing when feelings and money are interdependent; you need to prioritize what is more important for you and only then to make your choice.

Health. Your energy levels are quite high this month and the stars advise you only to channel your energy into peaceful purposes.

LIBRA

Try not to cut corners. You need to make steady progress towards your goals at the moment. This is true for both work and for love.

Business. In the professional sphere, you are facing a busy and yet very important period. Many Librans will have to solve a number of really complicated problems. There will be many organisational issues related to land, real estate or other large property and the solution involves facing down the vehement hostility of your opponents, competitors and spiteful others.

Such conflicts are possible for the whole month and they will be impossible to sort out without the help of mediators who turn up closer to the end of July or in August. Although the problem will only be completely resolved closer to December, it will be worth it. So, roll up your sleeves and get down to it!

Clerical workers are likely to face some changes and some serious rivalry in their company. The stars suggest paying careful attention to all your duties at work and, if necessary, asking some friendly higher-ups for help - there will be such a possibility for you.

Money. Despite a number of professionally related situations, you will not have any money problems. All of your costs and expenses are sensible and predictable.

You will receive a good amount of money in the first days of the month, between the 9th and the 11th, and on the 19th and 20th of July.

Love and family. Those whose interests are concentrated in their personal lives will also have to endure a stressful period. Families will have constant arguments with the main reason for conflict being real estate or other large property.

In a number of situations, there will be problems related to divorce and to the division of property. In other less serious scenarios, conflicts may be caused by relatives, parents or some senior family members and again, real estate or some large property may be at issue.

Health. Your energy levels are quite high this month and there is no need to worry about your health.

SCORPIO

In July you are likely to face serious changes at work, in your relationships and even in your ways of thought and behavior. It is likely that you will need to remind yourself of the Chinese saying, 'God save us from living in times of change' more than a few times this month.

Business. You will be full of get up and go this month. However, the stars highly recommend avoiding hasty and rash decisions.

Those who have relationships with colleagues from other cities and overseas will be faced with difficulty more than once. The problems might be legal ones that seriously affect your ambitious plans and projects; red tape that you must work away at for almost the entire month. This includes those who plan to move to a different city or abroad and to start a business there.

Entrepreneurs, managers and clerical workers should prepare for possible unexpected inspections and checks this month; or possibly for the re-emergence of some old legal problems.

Money. Financially, the situation in July looks really unstable; this is not surprising given your professional situation. There will be a slight change in the situation closer to the end of the month and you can expect a large amount of money on the 29th or 30th of July.

Love and family. Those whose interests focus on their personal lives will also be faced with problems this month. Principally, this involves your relationships with your close relatives. There might be a serious conflict involving the whole family, a family member might go through difficult times or fall seriously ill; all of these affect you personally.

Those who are moving to faraway places will also face some problems - some red tape or other serious obstacles. You should tackle these various difficulties step by step and remember the saying, 'slow and steady wins the race'. The sky will clear in August and your positions will be strengthened closer to September.

Health. Even though your energy levels are quite high this month, the stars highly recommend being more careful during trips and while driving. In this respect, the whole month looks very inauspicious, especially the first twenty days. The stars therefore recommend canceling long-distance trips completely.

SAGITTARIUS

Material things and values will be of primary importance for you during this quite complicated month. Again, however, you will prove to be a rock.

Business. In July, many Sagittarians will have to part with a large amount of money or property. This may be related either to major purchases or to some unexpected losses. In any case you should be careful and cautious and not make any hasty decisions in the first half of the month - being too hasty at this time is surely a big mistake!

This is true for those who plan to invest in business development or to buy plots of land or real estate. It is better to spend the first 15 days of July analyzing, choosing and preparing your future actions and reserving the important decisions for the second part of July.

Your relationships with your partners are quite docile in this period although you might have some minor financial disagreements and misunderstandings caused by differing views on the future of your business. Looking further ahead, we might suggest that most of your problems will be successfully resolved in a month's time.

Money. Financially, July will be quite costly to you. Money will haemorrhage incessantly due to your business or your personal life and the needs of family and children - you should bear in mind that there will be quite a number of needs.

Love and family. Many families will become concerned about household problems; not necessarily in their own household. Many of your birth sign will have to help their children either with school fees or possibly with purchasing real estate.

For lovers this month is difficult, especially if you have duties to other people where you have to solve not only moral questions but financial problems. Most of the situations will be sorted out by the middle of August, but you must make the effort now and resolve the problems one by one.

Health. Your energy levels are not high this month. Those who are medically vulnerable and the elderly should be extra careful. You should be careful about the quality of the food you eat and not strain yourself unnecessarily. There is a high possibility of injury, accident and other unpleasant situations on the road this month.

CAPRICORN

You might experience pressure from all sides in July, but you will hold the line. Without doubt, the decisions on many matters are in your hands!

Business. Professionally active Capricorns, along with their business partners, will have to sort out a situation that is quite complicated and rooted in the past. This will possibly be related to real estate, land or other large property.

The situation looks unpredictable in the first half of the month: it will be quite difficult to understand your opponents' demands as they dodge and weave and alter their game-plan. The situation will settle in the second half of July and your partners' demands will become clearer.

However, you are unlikely to be able to meet your opponents' expectations and so there is likely to be more discussion, argument and conflict. The situation is more likely to be resolved in August or September than this month. Nevertheless, your position is the stronger and the final terms and conditions of any agreements therefore depend totally on you. Your relationships with colleagues from other cities and overseas are developing quite well, and even if some delays are possible in the first half of the month, they do not cause any great complications in the scheme of things.

Money. Financially, this month is mainly neutral with all your earnings and expenses being quite sensible and predictable.

Love and family. Those lucky enough to escape professional problems will be caught up in difficulties in their personal life - mainly in the family. Unhappy spouses might have frequent arguments, which in the worst case leads to discussion of divorce and in turn to financial problems and questions of accommodation. It is unlikely that you can solve this problem peacefully and you will certainly be unable to reach any compromise this month. August and September look calmer and more promising and so you will hopefully come to some sort of agreement then.

Lovers will be in a better situation as it is possible that the stormy July will pass you by.

Health.
Your energy levels are not high this month, but if you remember about the benefits of sleeping well and spending more time outdoors, you might be able to avoid any health issues.

AQUARIUS

July is quite difficult. The main trend is a large amount of work that brings neither joy nor pleasure.

Business. As the first half of the month is an unclear and quite tense time, you should not plan anything important for this period. It is likely that you will still be fighting off various problems from last month.

Entrepreneurs and managers might become the object of an over-zealous interest from the authorities. The stars highly recommend that you prepare for inspections as you are unlikely to be happy with the results otherwise. It is possible that some information emerges which really should have been kept secret.

Those whose business is connected with colleagues from other cities and overseas might experience some complications. Various misunderstandings, emergencies or legal problems are possible.

Clerical workers might find it very difficult to work in an environment where there is conflict or even poisonous assignation within the body of staff. In the worst-case scenario, it might even come to their dismissal.

Managers of all levels should keep their employees on a tight leash because their work is far from perfect.

Money. Financially, the situation looks neutral. Money will come in as it did last month and nothing unexpected will happen, at least for the time being.

Love and family. Those whose focus is their personal life will suffer some difficult times. There might be some serious problems with your relatives – an argument or other issues with your closest relatives. Some of your close relatives might fall ill and you will have to take an active part in their treatment.

Looking further ahead, we may say that most of your current problems will be sorted out in August and the rest in September.
Lovers might unexpectedly fall out or not see each other as often as they would like.

All Aquarians should be alert that some unpleasant secrets might emerge in July.

Health. Those who luckily escape professional and personal troubles might have problems with their health. Take care and visit a good physician if necessary but under no circumstances should you self-medicate.

You should also be careful while driving and during trips. Avoid dangerous situations as the possibility of accident and injury is quite high this month.

pisces

*You might be at peace neither with yourself nor with others
in your circle this month. You should control yourself!*

Business. Professionally active Pisceans will have some serious problems with friends and some high-ranking officials this month; possible reasons might well be money and other material concerns. It is impossible to resolve all the disputed situations straight away; you will be dealing with them not only in July but for the most part of August.

Those in creative occupations might find the situation especially difficult. They are at risk of losing everything – money, popularity and promoters. So, think twice before taking any steps and act only after you have considered all the pros and cons.

Everyone of your birth sign should not take irreversible decisions in the first half of the month. Mercury is moving backwards in this period and therefore it is not a good time to sign paperwork, meet new people or make final decisions. The stars recommend waiting until the time is ripe;

taking things as they come and avoiding emotional, impulsive actions. This advice is true not only for your work but also for your personal relationships.

Money. The financial situation looks quite unstable in July. You will experience a constant draining away of money; sometimes related to your work and sometimes to your personal life. In any case you should be more careful of the people around you and not lend money - even to your closest friends - as it might result in a serious problem later.

Love and family. The tough times continue in your personal life. Parents will be busy solving their children's problems and we can observe that, 'the older the child, the more serious their problems'. In all events one thing is true – a very substantial amount of money might need to be spent on your children's needs this month.

If you have a conflict with your children, you should be more tactful and thoughtful. It might be that the problem is not only with your children's behavior, but with yours.

For most lovers this is also a difficult month. The situation might be so complicated that you are unable to untangle it this month. You should be patient and not make any hasty decisions in the first half of the month. Do not rush! It is never too late to have the last word; it is more important not to feel sorry about it later.

Health. Your energy levels are quite high this month and there is nothing to worry about except the nervous strain.

ARIES

August will be one of 2020's more unusual months. You will be constantly juggling home and work, and it is hard to say which is the more important to you this month. However, you are a tough nut to crack and the sky is the limit!

Business. Everything progresses nice and briskly although perhaps not exactly in the right direction. The problem is that, despite your energy and positive attitude, you are not immune to mistakes and failures. So, don't risk too much and don't make any hasty decisions; even if you should feel like it. Mars is in your birth sign making you short or even rude with people, and this could cause conflicts and misunderstandings.

You should remember that many situations can be sorted out peacefully and tactfully - this is true both for clerical workers and managers of all levels.

During the month you might experience conflict with high-up officials due to your rigid and unyielding stance. If you do not or cannot change your inflexible attitude, the problems will snowball as your opponent is not going to cede ground either.

Money. Financially, August might be unstable. Your expenses will only be followed by cash inflows with the largest amount arriving closer to the end of the month.

Love and family. The situation in your personal life is quite harmonious.

116

August is the month when many of your sign will find the time communicate with children, close relatives and friends and this is likely to happen somewhere far from home.

This is an ideal time for shopping; for buying something big and expensive. If you have planned to renew your wardrobe or to change your hairstyle, now is the best time to do so. Many of your birth sign will become welcome guests at various parties, birthday celebrations and other special occasions.

Single people might meet somebody interesting and pursue an exciting affair.

Nevertheless, the stars recommend being softer and more tactful in your personal relationships because the energy that Mars gives you this month may play a dirty trick on you. Remember that other people also have their own views on life and if you can learn to iron out these differences, August will be much more peaceful and enjoyable for you.

Health. Your energy levels are quite high in August, but you should only use this energy for peaceful purposes.

TAURUS

August is a more peaceful month when compared to earlier ones. You have a chance to stop and breathe, to reflect and to stiffen your spine.

Business. Professionally active Taureans will be able to slowly and calmly sort out a complicated, existing situation; everything is now clear but still not so easy.

Some may be concerned about legal matters, others about troubles with colleagues from other cities and overseas or complications with inspecting authorities. If you do happen to find yourself in such a situation, you should do everything in your power to clear it up. Even though it is unlikely to be completely resolved, you can nevertheless address many of the key elements. You should use all the opportunities with which August presents you because things will become drawn out and complicated in the fall your opportunity for action becomes severely limited.

Many of you will deal with real estate problems which are likely to be in a different city or abroad.

Money. The financial situation in August looks mainly neutral. You can expect neither big gains nor losses. Nevertheless, the astrologer advises you to be more practical and manage both your business and family budgets carefully as things might become more unpredictable in the fall.

Love and family. In your personal life, you will be able to spend more time at home - arranging or rearranging your household to make the lives of your close family members more comfortable. Your relationships with your relatives still cannot be described as ideal, but a window of opportunity opens in August which allows you to at least treat the situation more objectively. You should make the most of this because the window might close again in the middle of September.

Those who are moving faraway will be able to make improvements to their new home. This period is altogether an ideal one for sorting out many domestic issues.

Health. Your energy levels are not high in August, so try to find time for sleep or at least a good rest. You should solve problems as they come and be careful while driving and during trips as the possibility of injury this month is still high!

GEMINI

August is a busy and dynamic month. You will spend most of it dealing with various matters and will be able to achieve a lot.

Business. Some of the problems that worried you last month will be sorted out this month. These might be financial problems related to friends, co-workers or with some high-up officials. There might be negotiations that partially soften any reciprocal claims, but it is unlikely that you will be able to completely resolve everything. However, it is better than nothing and you should grab the chance given to you. In some cases, mediation in disputed matters might be carried out by relatives or colleagues from other cities or overseas. You should use all opportunities given to you now because the situation might deteriorate closer to the end of September or in the late fall.

Money. Despite a number of professional problems, the financial situation is stable. Money will arrive regularly and the approximate dates for the arrival of large sums are from the 5th to the 7th, the 15th and 16th and the 23rd to the 25th of August.

There will also be quite a lot of expenses which are in some cases related to your work and in others to your personal life; to problems with your family and home.

Love and family. Change continues in your personal life, possibly involving a new home improvement project or preparations for moving to a new place. Your relatives will play a significant part in all your household and domestic matters and their support - both moral and financial - will smooth over many past, present and future difficulties.

A trip planned for this month might improve relations between lovers and spouses.

Couples who fell out last month have a good chance to make up and they should take this chance because such a window of opportunity doesn't open very often.

You should solve the problems delicately and tactfully, bearing in mind that different people inevitably have different views on life and events.

Health. You are healthy and full of energy this month and you should be able to cope with anything that life throws at you.

CANCER

The last month of summer brings significant improvement to your work and personal life. You will be able to get your own way and to achieve the desired results.

Business. A complicated situation with partners will improve, at least partly. We cannot talk about a complete resolution of the argument at the moment - the future proves this - but you can still obtain some form of compensation this month and you take use this opportunity.

Your relationships with colleagues from other cities and overseas are developing well and you might have a trip where you could meet new partners towards the end of the month.

Clerical workers will continue to face changes at work, and this will turn out to be a long-term situation.

If you feel like changing jobs, it is better to successfully negotiate a decent package and do so now - it is unlikely to be possible come the fall.

Money. Many of your birth sign will observe, with some satisfaction, an improvement in their financial situation by the end of the month. The possible reasons are repaid debts, earnings at work and other payments.

You will not have many expenses in August and they all will be sensible and predictable.

Love and family. The situation in your personal life will improve slightly. There is unfortunately no suggestion of making-up completely; lovers and spouses in troubled relationships are still at each other's throats, but the number of incidents will reduce. The influence of Venus, who comes into your sign on the 7th of August, means you are more tactful and reasonably minded than your partner.

In many families, relatives will act as peacemakers and mediators for warring spouses not only in August but also in September.

Health. Your energy levels are not high this month. You need to take a break from your struggles and have some rest; this should be possible in the last ten days of August and at the beginning of September.

LEO

It is right for you to strive to be in charge for the whole of August. Who else if not you?

Business. You need patience and self-assurance for the long haul. You should stick to your business plan calmly and correct any mistakes as you find them. Your self-confidence is more prominent and inspiring to others than any facts at the moment and, thanks to this, you will be able to resolve some of the matters that concerned you in July.

A difficult situation with colleagues from other cities and overseas will improve and there might be constructive negotiations and a successful trip. Any legal problems and tangled situations resulting from audits and inspections by the authorities will become clearer.

The situation will surely improve but you should not expect it to clear up completely as complications will arise again during the fall. Nevertheless, August represents a golden opportunity for you to turn the situation around, at least partly, and you should grab it with both hands.

Many Leos will receive interesting new proposals and good money at the end of the month.

Money. The financial situation will improve remarkably, especially at the end of the month. You might receive good money between the 10th and the 12th, and on the 20th, 28th and 29th of August.

Love and family. You should not expect to make great strides in your personal life but relationships with some of your relatives will improve somewhat. The situation will improve for close relatives who fell ill or went through a bad patch. Complications are still possible, but to a lesser extent if compared to July.

Lovers who have had problems in the past might be busy licking their wounds and considering the vexing question of whether to remain in the relationship or not. When solving this very personal matter, you should not only take all the possibilities into account but also to try to get more of a feel for the situation.

Health. Energy levels for most Leos will improve significantly in August, and even those who fell ill last month will gradually begin to fully recover.

VIRGO

If you have prepared a to-do list for this month, get rid of it without hesitation. The best thing you can do is dig in.

Business. Sorting out recent problems will occupy you for most of August. Mainly, this will be a complicated situation with friends or some of your co-workers related to money or other property. It is likely that you will be able to smooth the waters this month but unfortunately, despite some successful negotiations, you will not be able to completely resolve the issue. You should, however, take this chance now because you will not get another one during the fall.

Your relationships with colleagues from other cities and overseas develop with varying degrees of success - some things will work out and some things will not. There will be some good news at the end of August, however. There might also be a successful business trip where you could meet interesting new partners in this period.

Money. August will be quite a ruinous time, as was July. Money will just ooze away and it's possible that this will not be a short-lived phenomenon. This is why you should not only tighten your belt but hold the purse strings of your relatives.

Those who are finance professionals should be extra prudent as the possibility of mistakes and resulting financial loss is quite high this month. Those not in business might spend money on the needs of family members, children and close relatives.

Love and family. Processes that have already begun in your personal life continue this month. Families will still have to spend money on their children, and this is likely to remain true for the whole of the fall.

Conflicts with some of your friends will continue. If the problem is over debt or other liability, you might not get your money back, either in whole or part. Conversely, if it is you who is indebted, it is more than likely that you will have to repay everything.

Lovers will go through a period of loneliness. If you have had an argument in the past, you might still be suffering from the repercussions. You might be able to make up with each other, but future events might prove this to be a fragile and insincere reconciliation.

Health. In the first twenty days of August, you should take care of yourself and stick to your limits - your energy levels are not high. This is a good time for self-care, therapy and long walks in the fresh air.

LIBRA

Your struggle goes on, but it may now take on a different - less aggressive and more diplomatic - nature.

Business. You will take a strong stand in August and you will ask friends, associates and allies for their help in achieving your goals. Among them will be highly respected members of society who act as mediators and are able to quell a recent dispute. Friendly negotiations are quite possible, although the result is likely an unpredictable one. Soon, however, your opponents will return to their objections and begin to voice their disagreement in their old defiant and aggressive manner. This time you must do everything in your power to enlist support from friends, associates and others interested in seeing you prevail in future.

Major real estate, property or land is still at stake and if we look further ahead, we see that you do retain it, but only after rows, conflicts and real confrontation.

Money. The financial situation in August is quite stable; both earnings and expenses are sensible and predictable this month.

Love and family. The situation in your personal life is still complicated. The stars highly recommend you to tame the spirit of defiance which is characteristic of you this month and be more open to the opinions of your friends or close relatives. Rest or sharing mutual concerns about children might soothe the situation for spouses in some troubled relationships. If you plan to save your marriage, you should use the chances given to you in August. On the other hand, if you have no such plans, there is no need to take heed of these recommendations.

In the case of divorce and a complicated divorce settlement, there comes an unexpected opportunity to sort everything out nearer to the end of August. You should take the opportunity because there will be no further chances during the fall. Your partner could easily break any oral agreements and, knowing this, you should make sure to have written, legal documents about any agreement.

Friendly couples might overcome various difficulties related to real estate or property disputes.

Health. Your energy levels are quite high in August and there is no need to worry about your health.

SCORPIO

In August you will be able to square the circle – to combine patience and enthusiasm. With such a combination, you can expect to make if not the breakthrough you want, then at least a temporary advance.

Business. August is a good time to find new allies, assistants and patrons and this is good news for you because the problems of recent months are still hanging over you and need to be resolved.

Do not hesitate to set yourself particular goals in August and in the first ten days of September because there is a good chance of improving a difficult prior situation which is possibly related to your long-term relationships with colleagues from far away.

Those who plan on starting a business in a different city or abroad closer to the end of the month might meet new people who are able to sort out some of their organizational questions.

Clerical workers will be able to improve their relationship with their management team and this will, in turn, significantly improve their relations with colleagues. We can also say that while any petty intrigues recede for a time, they do not disappear completely yet but possibly linger on into October and the first half of November.

Money. The financial situation will improve to some extent and you might expect large amounts of money to arrive on the 17th, 18th, and the 27th to the 29th of August.

Love and family. Your personal life might turn out to be of less importance than work. Although many families will continue having problems with relatives, these can at least be soothed this month.

There might be serious arguments or other major issues in the circles of your closest relatives. In both cases, old friends and new acquaintances, who are likely to appear at the end of August or in the first ten days of September, will help.

Single people and those who have been disappointed by former relationships can expect to meet someone with whom something significant might develop in the future.

Health. Your energy levels are quite high for the whole month and you will be resistant to most illnesses. Nevertheless, the stars recommend being more careful while driving and during any trips.

SAGITTARIUS

Most of this month is quite favorable. You will be able to recover the balance which you thought you had lost some time ago. This is true in both your working life and your love life.

125

Business. The situation concerning your professional matters improves significantly and this will become especially noticeable towards the end of the month. During this period there might be new proposals and contracts which are interesting from both a professional and a financial point of view.

You may have to spend the first part of August sorting out problems from the past and these might be disputes with partners or financial claims from opponents. With the help of your allies, your assistants and, of course, the stars you can relieve the pressure to make it less acute and painful.
It is possible that you will receive both moral and financial help from colleagues from other cities and overseas. A successful business trip is also possible this month.

Money. The financial situation will become noticeably better towards the end of August and moreover, this favorable trend will last into September. You will have some expenses this month related either to work or to your personal life; to the needs of your family and home.

Love and family. The situation in your personal life will also improve. Families will succeed in resolving some problems related to their children and although you will still have to spend some money on their needs, this will be less than it has been.

Spouses going through a divorce will be able to reach a compromise regarding the up-bringing, education and future of their offspring.

Lovers at odds with each other have a good opportunity to rebuild their relationship. To make a journey somewhere together would be a great chance to forget old demands and festering resentments. This advice is also good for married couples where relations are far from ideal.

August also offers an excellent opportunity to discuss all your problems and you should do so because disputes might rear their head again in the fall.

Health. Your energy levels will significantly improve this month and even those who fell ill last month will soon recover. August is perfect for taking care of yourself; for receiving treatments somewhere far from home; for going to a spa and for all types of cosmetic procedures - including plastic surgery.

CAPRICORN

Your extremely strong intuition in August enables you to cut corners in your relationships with partners; both business and personal. Compromise is the keyword for the last month of summer.

Business. It would undoubtedly be better to spend August resting and working on personal issues but if you are a hopeless workaholic, you will have no problem with working to put your matters in order and to solve issues in your relationships with certain colleagues and opponents.

If you are faced with a dispute over real estate and land, there is a good chance of fixing this in August. Although you should not expect to completely resolve it, you will still be able to discuss the most burning issues amicably. While it is quite possible that you can placate your more hostile opponents, you must be more flexible and less demanding in return.

The perfect time for this is the second part of August and the first half of September and you should use all the given opportunities now because the situation more or less repeats itself in the fall.

Any trips planned for this period stand a good chance of being very successful.

Money. The financial situation will not be very stable for most of August. You will experience a constant drain of money related to either work or to your personal life.

Love and family. The situation also improves in your personal life. Spouses who are going through a divorce might reach a compromise acceptable to both parties. It is possible that the short-term solution is money, but this will be only temporary. Despite heavy expenditure, your partner might repeat their demands and the fall of 2020 looks quite problematic in this respect.

Happy couples will solve disputed real estate problems together. It is also likely that you will be involved in a long and serious renovation.

For lovers, this month is quite neutral. Some unpleasant news about your loved one might turn up at the very beginning of the month that causes complications in your relationship. The astrologer sees a minor disagreement or even a temporary split. The situation will be fixed closer to the end of the month when you are likely to travel somewhere together and eventually make up.

Health. Your energy levels are not high for most of August. You might frequently feel tired and lethargic and the best treatment for this is proper rest and a good night's sleep.

August is a perfect time to improve your health by visiting a resort or spa. If you spend time taking care of yourself, you will benefit.

AQUARIUS

Do not try to solve all your problems by yourself. The Arab saying, 'one hand cannot clap' is an appropriate one for August.

Business. August is a good time to somehow solve the problems of recent months which either relate to inspections or legal problems or to situations with colleagues from other cities and overseas.

In any case, you will be able to alleviate the situation but only by addressing your allies or other competent consultants.

You should use all the opportunities presented to you and tackle the problems step by step; cautiously and prudently. Although you cannot expect complete success, you will be able to achieve much, and this is better than nothing.

Real estate deals continue and you might expect a genuine breakthrough at the end of August or in the first ten days of September. During this period, you might receive some new proposals and many of the issues that have been bothering you will quickly be resolved.

Money. The financial situation is not quite stable for the first twenty days of August whereas the last week of the month and the first week of September will be more successful. During this period, you might profit from beneficial real estate transactions or the receipt of a loan. Those not involved in business might expect the support of parents or loved ones.

Love and family. The situation in your personal life will also improve. Complications between close relatives become more understandable and easier to solve as a result. It is possible that your spouse or partner will help you with the more difficult issues and also with situations when your relatives are faced with troubles or serious mischief.

Happily married couples might be busy solving problems connected with either purchasing or selling real estate.

Health. Your energy levels are not high this month, so you need to take care of yourself, hustle less and remember the benefits of a good's sleep.

You should be cautious when traveling and driving as there is still the risk of accident and injury.

pisces

You will be busy in August doing things you really don't want to do but must. Don't make a mountain out of a molehill, however, as you have both the strength and capability to cope!

Business. You will have lots of work. This will positively affect your financial situation and in turn help to solve some of the difficulties you happen to find yourself in. You will, however, still have to deal with complications in your relationships with some of your friends, co-workers or higher-ups. The core of your argument is a financial disagreement and you now have a chance to partly remedy the situation in August before finally solving it completely in the future.

Your relationships with colleagues from other cities and overseas develop well and this will become most noticeable towards the end of August. You will have a successful business trip where you can establish new and useful relationships in the last week of August or in the first ten days of

September.

Money. The financial situation will improve as a result of your good past and present work. You will have a regular inflow of money and the approximate dates for receiving good money in August are the 1st, 2nd, 8th, 9th, the 17th to the 19th, the 26th and the 27th.

There will also be quite a lot of expense related either to your work or to your personal life.

You might have old debts repaid to you this month and this will subsequently allow you to square accounts with your creditors.

Love and family. Processes in your personal life which have already started will continue this month. Parents are likely to have problems with children and face the corresponding expenses.

Spouses might have frequent arguments and a possible reason for this might be differing views on your children's future up-bringing and development.

Lovers are also likely to have misunderstandings. In the most complicated cases, the real reason for this is money or other financial problems. In other cases, the reason for conflict might be differing outlooks on life and contrasting values. It will be a little bit easier at the end of August and in the first ten days of September when you are likely to travel, meet new people and have fresh experiences; all of which can help improve relations between lovers and spouses.

Those who have been disappointed by previous relationships might meet somebody interesting in this period; either during a trip or among those who have come from far away.

Health. Your energy levels are not high in August. This is therefore a good time for resting at a health resort, for renewing your wardrobe or even for changing your entire image. Don't be afraid to choose what is best for you!

SEPTEMBER

ARIES

Try not to jump the gun and cause any serious situations. If you are to achieve your goals, you need to move step by step and adhere to the old saying, 'slow and steady wins the race'.

Business. September will be a busy and active month. The positives are the clear progress in your professional activities and some accompanying financial achievements. Entrepreneurs and managers of all levels can depend on their employees and trust them with important tasks.

While clerical workers will be pleased to receive the support of their colleagues, communication with their management team and other higher authorities could falter. There might be conflicts caused by the recent problems and it might even be you who rocks the boat with your lack of tact and flexibility.

The stars recommend trying not to exacerbate the situation - no matter how confident you are and how strongly you feel. At present, those above you are stronger than you and their stance will remain entrenched; especially if you try to pressure them or take the path to confrontation. You should therefore change your approach to take a low-key, professional approach where sound reasoning is backed up by hard facts - only then will you be heard and understood correctly. These recommendations are true both for clerical workers and businessmen.

Money. The financial situation is quite stable. You will have regular cash inflows with a noticeable increase in the amount. However, you never get something for nothing in this life and so you will have to work really hard this month.

The approximate dates for receiving larger amounts of money are the 2nd, the 6th to the 8th, the 16th, 17th, 24th and 25th of September.

Love and family. If you have had problems in your personal life in recent months, you should prepare yourself for their re-occurrence in September. You might become irritated with your partner and their present attitude and the first week of the month will be especially difficult with past tensions blooming into serious clashes; the situation will improve towards the end of September but may well recur again later. You should be patient and try not to ignite any conflicts; especially if you cherish your partner and hope to stay together.

Health. Your energy levels are not high this month, so take good care of yourself and keep to your limits. September is a good time to visit a spa or a beauty salon. It is also good for you to keep yourself active and spend more time outdoors at the weekends.

TAURUS

September is an unstable and quite contentious month for you. The positive and negative influences of the stars intermingle; you will have to maneuver hard to avoid problems and take advantage of any favorable opportunities.

Business. There will be a chance to alleviate a previous issue in September, at least partially. It may be trouble with colleagues from other cities and overseas, aged legal problems or disagreements over inspections. In any case, the situation can be improved with money, by using your connections or in other possible ways. Looking further ahead, we can say that the problem is too complicated to be completely resolved in the short-term. Do not give up, however, tackle the problem step by step, be careful in your actions and remember the old saying, 'a journey of thousand miles begins with a single step'.

Money. This month will not be easy financially. You will experience a regular leakage of money due to your work or to your personal life. The stars highly recommend you to carefully assess the reliability of those you deal with and to be very wary of those making promises - the astrologer has good grounds to believe that most of these promises are false ones.

Love and family. Problems in your personal life that began in the past also continue. These problems mainly concern your relationships with your relatives and the difficulties in this area may persist for a few more months; coming and going like the tide. In some cases, children might act as the doves of peace and their participation in family matters is definitely beneficial.

Those who are moving to faraway places will continue to overcome the various resulting difficulties with paperwork, bureaucracy or the law.

Health. Your energy levels are quite high in September and you should not worry about your health. Nevertheless, the stars highly recommend being more careful while traveling and while driving - the possibility of an accident or other unpleasant incident on the road is still high in September.

GEMINI

Like a good general before a campaign, you should use September to halt, regroup and reinforce.

Business. Sometimes in life we have to do things we do not like and most of September is just such a time. You will have to patiently work through the problems of recent months step by step. These problems might be conflicts with friends and high-up officials or disagreements among your co-workers. This time, however, you will be able to enlist the support of friends and close relatives whose help will be timely and effective. Because many of the problems this month are of a financial nature, their financial support is quite possible. It is unlikely, however, that all of the sensitive issues will be fixed this month and the solution may continue to elude you. Furthermore, you will have to expend a lot of time and effort to conclude this undesirable chapter.

Money. The financial situation looks more positive compared to recently, and this includes not only your own, personal money. Your financial situation will improve because of financial support from some of your partners, loans or lines of credit and you might also profit from successful real estate deals.

Those not involved in business will receive support from close relatives; either parents or spouses.

Builders and those in construction and real estate will be especially lucky this month.

Love and family. Many Gemini will have major events in their home and within their family this month. You are likely to be faced with serious change such as moving house, a change in your marital status or the social standing of your family. You might also have to take steps to prepare any necessary arrangements.

Relationships between lovers are still not perfect, and again this is due to recent problems. Judging by the intensity of emotions, however, there is still a connection between you; otherwise there would be nothing left to play for.

A further acute conflict is possible at the beginning of the month, but the situation will become more peaceful again towards the end of the month.

Health. Your energy levels are not high this month, so you need to remember that September is known to be a bit of a low season and is thus a good time to enjoy a holiday.

CANCER

September is quite a frustrating month. On the one hand, you are very active and likely to do many things. On the other hand, you are unlikely to achieve your main goals. This in no way means that you should give up, however.

Business. The main achievement this month is the development of partnerships with your colleagues from other cities and overseas. With the assistance of both new and existing contacts, you might be able to settle a recent dispute you have had with some of your partners.

As the problem is so complex, you will not be able to completely resolve it this month and it is very possible that the current situation drags on into the future. Nevertheless, peaceful negotiations are possible, and you should make full use of this opportunity. The old saying, 'make love, not war' is always true and especially so for you now.

Clerical workers might witness a changing situation at work. It might be a change of management, a reorganisation or even the shuttering of the business. You should pay attention to all events because the changes will come to affect your own interests in due time. If the worst comes to the worst, you might try to find a different outlet for your talents.

Money. The financial situation will improve slightly; your income will increase and this will allow you to be more confident and optimistic about the future. The approximate dates for receiving good money this month are the 4th, 5th, 14th, 15th, 22nd, 23rd, 28th and 29th.

Love and family. The situation in your personal life will become calmer and more even. Although relatives will somehow manage to reconcile the conflict between spouses, the main underlying reason for the misunderstandings, either real estate or other property, remains. If spouses are involved in business together, the situation will only worsen.

In other words, you will have a multitude of problems this month and you will have to navigate them carefully in order for the situation not to become terminal. If you do actually split up, there is a strong possibility of the worst happening. If you are reading this well in advance, you should try to safeguard your situation as it might become difficult to do so later.

Relationships with your relatives are strengthening. Indeed, you might meet your relatives from a different city or abroad - maybe you will travel to them or they will travel to you.

The situation between lovers will improve and a possible journey together will make the relationship stronger.

Health. Your energy levels are quite high this month and there is no need to worry about your health.

Leo

Your discipline, persistence and ambition guide well you in September; these qualities allow you to cope with most recent difficulties.

Business. Professionally active Leos have good opportunities to reinforce their position in September. After some of the serious shocks with which you had to cope over the summer, it might seem that a quiet and predictable period has started in your life; this might turn out to be a very unstable and fragile illusion, however. Both this month and a little further on, you will face a number of unpleasant situations related either to legal problems or to the incessant attentions of the authorities and their inspections.

As usual, entrepreneurs and managers should pay attention to their employees and clerical workers to their colleagues. The situation remains tense in many companies.

Nevertheless, your business will continue to develop despite the difficulties, and this will have an effect on your financial situation.

Money. Many of your sign will see, with some satisfaction, that their financial situation has noticeably improved in September. You will have a lot more money and the approximate dates for the arrival of large sums of money are the 6th to the 8th, the 16th, 17th and the 24th to the 26th of September. You will still have plenty of expenses, however; most of which will be related to fixing problems in your personal and your professional life.

Love and family. Many families will continue to have problems with relatives. There might be a long-term rift that seems endless and intractable or you might find yourself having to take on your relative's problems personally and assist them with both word and deed.

Health. Due to the influence of Venus who is lodged in your sign this month, your energy levels will increase to some extent, but you cannot lower your guard. If you have recently had some health problems, you should not neglect your health as doing so might lead to a recurrence of the illness and this might be really difficult to cope with. Remember this and take good care of yourself.

Again, drivers and those traveling should be cautious, as the possibility of accidents and unpleasant situations remains.

VIRGO

You will finally be able to breathe easily in September. For the first time after the difficult summer months, you start to feel confident and to understand that, no matter what the problem, there is always a way out.

Business. The main achievement this month is the cultivation of contacts; either new people who appear from over the horizon or renewed relationships with former partners. Your relationships with colleagues from other cities and overseas develop well and you might have a successful trip this month.

However, together with the positive events of September, you will have to deal with a number of problems left over from the summer. There may be complicated relationships with some of your friends, partners or co-workers or troubles with some high-ranking official. All of the above-mentioned problems might be of a financial nature and persist for quite a time to come.

Because you can only deal with a fraction of the whole situation this month, it can hardly be described as a totally successful month for you.

Money. The financial situation in September is really difficult. You will experience a regular draining away of money caused either by work or by your personal life and the needs of your children, family and home.

Love and family. The situation in your personal life looks more rational and tranquil this month. Families will be able to partly remedy a complicated situation with their children, but will be unable to completely solve it this month; some questions will come up this month, others will only come up a little later. In any case, you will need all of your energies and money to resolve the whole situation. However, who else could do it but you?

Lovers will find themselves in a more complicated situation - you take a step towards your partner and you seem to get a response, but their demands on you do not lessen. You will unfortunately be faced with such issues this month and subsequently.

Health. Although you feel stronger and more energetic this month, it should not be taken as an excuse to take risks and experiment with your health. Mars will be in the danger zone of your chart for a long time yet and this means that you should be cautious in everything that you do – driving, using domestic appliances or indeed any potentially hazardous situation.

LIBRA

Despite the pressure of your circumstances, you are determined in pursuit of your goal. If it is worth it, it is worth fighting for!

Business. You will spend most of September on large-scale organization. Entrepreneurs and various managers will be busy doing just this and will succeed in many of their tasks. It is fine to plan further operations on real estate or land whose ownership is disputed; the conflicts continue but they will not lead you off your path. Looking further ahead, one might imagine that you do not win consent in the future either and so you should act according to an old piece of Arab wisdom, 'the dogs may bark but the caravan goes on'.

Clerical workers could take a break from work and focus on some of their ever-growing personal matters.

Entrepreneurs and managers should still watch their employees carefully. Clerical workers should still be cautious of their colleagues. There might be various misunderstandings caused either by the dishonesty or the incompetence of certain people.

Money. The financial situation is fairly stable. You should expect neither to make large and successful gains nor to take serious damage. Taking everything into account, things are not as bad as they could be. You might have income from various real estate deals; this affects those who have a construction business or those who have business with plots of land, houses and flats.

Love and family. For many Librans, the main events of this month will happen at home and in the family. Unhappily married couples will continue their fractious behavior and there is no sign on the horizon of them making up.

Arguments and conflicts will continue to flare up from time to time, and the situation does seem serious. The main discussions are likely to be about a house, flat or other large property but your partner's position does look quite active and aggressive, however. In a different scenario, your partner might be faced with some serious troubles and you will need to help them with word and deed.

Health. Your energy levels are not high this month, so try not to hustle too much or let yourself get over-anxious about the challenges which life throws up at you; everything will happen in its own good time.

SCORPIO

The situation looks more positive this month - you have an opportunity to fix a problem and you should definitely take it!

Business. This month, you will meet some people who can either solve or at least dampen down some of your outstanding problems. You really should try to establish co-operation with them as the next month is going to be a difficult one and you will need any and all of the support that you can get.

There might be difficulties related to old legal problems, to complications with colleagues from other cities and overseas or to the activities of the authorities and their inspections. Old friends or high-ranking officials will suggest some ways out of this complicated situation but what decision you make is entirely up to you. Do not, however, be in too much of a hurry here! There are a few difficult months coming up and only then will the problem come to a head. You should consider all the possible variants and ask those who care about your future to help you. This is also true for clerical workers who find themselves in a difficult situation at work.

Money. Despite your professional problems, your financial situation improves in September. You cannot bank on any major achievements, but these are still nevertheless possible. Your expenses will be connected to services rendered by others and also to the needs of your family and children.

Love and family. Although you will also notice some improvements in your personal life, they may only be minor ones. For instance, your relationships with your relatives will improve a little bit and you can rely on the help of your some of your friends to facilitate this. In a different scenario, relatives who have been through some troubles will come out of the other side, and this in turn benefits the mood and feeling in the entire family.

Those of you moving somewhere far away will keep chipping away at your various difficulties with determination. After a string of quite serious problems, you will definitely prevail, but possibly only towards the end of the year. Most relationships between lovers are not ideal and this month is no exception; you are likely to be disappointed with each other and to fall out and it may even be that you are about to split up.

Health. Your energy levels are quite high this month and this will allow you to overcome the problems of the previous months.

Again, the stars recommend you be more careful while traveling and driving as the possibility of accidents and other unpleasant situations still remains high.

SAGITTARIUS

You will need to remind yourself of the old saying, 'the early bird catches the worm' many times in September. Your fortune is slowly revealing itself to you piece by piece. Go for it!

Business. Professionally, September is one of the best months for you. You have been working hard for a long time, saved money, obtained the necessary knowledge and prepared the documentation. It looks like you have everything ready and so you now have every chance to taste a brighter future.

This month brings new projects and new proposals that have good prospects and are very interesting from a financial point of view. Along with the positives there will also be some negatives, however. In many cases your recent problems with friends or high-ranking officials over money and other financial liabilities will continue. Looking further ahead, one might forecast this to be a long-term tendency and you will not be able to resolve all of these sensitive matters in September. Nevertheless, there are no problems which cannot be solved and in about two or three months, you will finally succeed in sorting everything out.

Money. The financial situation will improve significantly this month, and this helps to deal not only with many of September's problems but also those of many months ago.

The approximate dates in September when you might receive substantial amounts of cash are the 2nd, the 6th to the 8th, the 16th, 17th, 24th, 25th, 29th and the 30th.

You will still have a lot of expenses but the astrologer sees that most of your costs relate to your personal life; to your loved one and your children.

Love and family. Even if your professional situation looks quite positive, we cannot, unfortunately, say the same about your personal life. Many families will continue to have problems with children and they will be the cause of most of your expenses this month.

In some cases, your children will be faced with troubles that began some time ago and you will have to help them in word and in deed. In other cases, you will have to make a serious investment in the up-bringing and education of the younger generation.

The situation between lovers is still complicated. It might be that you have been dreaming of something but now come face to face with cold, hard reality. It might be that your partner has changed their plans or got themselves into a tricky and thorny situation. Life is not theatre and so you need to be more patient and accepting - this the best you can do at the moment.

Health. This month your energy levels are quite high and there is no need to worry about any problems with your health.

CAPRICORN

This month you have to decide if your circumstances match your desires. Are you ready to go through thick and thin to get what you want? If yes, go right ahead! If you have doubts, stop and weigh things up in your mind. This advice is true in both work and love.

Business. A complicated situation from the summer will become more understandable in September and consequently more resolvable. A disputed situation with some of your partners is still acute but there are possibilities to somehow calm it down at the moment; you might, for example, get some good legal support that makes your position more stable and if the question is over real estate or other large property, your opponents will have to then cede at least some ground. Nevertheless, as the struggle is not yet over you need to keep your powder topped up.

Your relations with colleagues from other cities and overseas develop well; you are likely to either travel yourself or to welcome visiting colleagues from far away.

Money. The financial situation is stable. You will have a regular inflow of cash and your expenses sensible and predictable.

Love and family. It is likely that most adversity this month relates to recent family problems.

Married couples continue to have troubles. Couples going through a divorce will have difficulties concerning the division of property; principally their main dwelling. While it is possible to carry out negotiations in September, it is likely that the counterparty will impede any amicable settlement. You should be ready for such a turn of events and remember that all family related issues require serious attention. This is true not only for couples going through a divorce but also for those whose relationship is far from perfect.

Lovers are in a slightly better position although they will have their own problems; this will be especially evident for those who like to play both sides.

The stars recommend that lovers and spouses go on a journey to help lower the temperature in the relationship from its current fever pitch and to give rise to more optimistic feelings about the future. This is also true for those whose relationship is still thriving.

Health. Your energy levels are high enough this month for you not to have to worry about falling ill.

AQUARIUS

September is a routine, working month. Take a breather!
Opportunities just around the corner might rock your world
and you need to be energized and prepared for them.

Business. It is better to rest and busy yourself with personal matters in September. However, if you are a workaholic, and your work always comes first, you can put your matters in order; carry out some organizational duties and fix any outstanding problems related to old legal issues and tensions with authorities and their inspections.

In a different scenario, the problems might lie in a long-standing conflict with colleagues from other cities or overseas or with paperwork and red tape. At present, all the issues are fundamental to your business and it is unlikely that you will be able to resolve them quickly.

Nevertheless, you will have to deal with the situation because you have no choice; it is quite serious and might require your attention once again in the near future.

Money. The financial situation is stable. You might have additional income from various real estate deals and from various lines of credit or easy-term loans.

You are very likely to come into an inheritance. Those involved in construction or the real estate and land industry will be especially successful.

Love and family. Many Aquarians will see the main events of September happen at home and in their family. There might be changes to the household, some of them only slight; perhaps finishing a permanent repair, a house-warming party or perhaps selling or exchanging a property.

Problems with your relatives continue. The astrologer sees these problems as being so serious that they cannot be resolved overnight; you will need to spend a few months working at these issues.

Lovers might suffer from the effects of rumor and gossip and the stars highly recommend safeguarding your relationship against any intrusion by strangers.

Health. Your energy levels are not high this month, so take care of yourself and keep to your limits. You should also be aware of the possibility of putting on weight, so remember the benefits of a balanced diet. You should also be more careful on trips and while driving as the possibility of accidents and unpleasant situations on the road is still there in September.

pisces

Relationship problems require your extra attention. You should state your opinion honestly and directly but also be ready to hear the reply.

Business. You will unexpectedly find allies this month and they might act as mediators between you and some of those with whom you have been disagreeing almost all summer. At some point you might think that you have reached a compromise, but it is not entirely true, however; the conflict will erupt again next month and you will face the exact same problem. Nevertheless, you need to use all the opportunities that September offers to you. Your present task is not to lose any more and to try to keep hold of what you already have - it is possible that we are talking here about large sums of money or a disputed property. The solution to this question might take long time and will be complicated but as the old saying goes, 'a journey of thousand miles begins with a single step'. Do not lose heart - deal with the problems logically and consistently.

This is all true for entrepreneurs and those with liabilities. Clerical workers have quite a successful period and they will be able to adjust their relationships with managers and colleagues as necessary.

Money. The financial situation is still complicated or, to be more exact, very unsteady. You will experience regular leaks of money either due to financial mismanagement or to your personal life.

Love and family. Those who have fortuitously escaped professional troubles will be confronted with problems in their personal life. Unhappily married couples will fight over communal property and probably also the futures of their children. Your partner may make some concessions towards you this month, but you need to consider them very carefully indeed.

If you delay and miss this opportunity, the situation will become worse for you. It goes without saying that this applies only to couples going through a divorce or those who are unhappily married. Those who are happily married will continue to deal with everyday problems and any complicated situations with their children together.

Lovers might find themselves in the uncertain situation where everything has been said but none of the parties can come to a decision. Perhaps it would be best not to decide right now but to let things run their course and see if the situation settles by itself – time will tell.

Health. Your energy levels are quite high this month and there is no need to worry about your health. Only in the last week of September will you feel a little tired and lethargic.

OCTOBER

ARIES

You will have to pay serious attention to the problems in your relationships. Even though you always follow the motto, 'all or nothing!', the stars recommend accepting some compromises at the moment.

Business. You are going through a most difficult period in business. Once again, entrepreneurs and managers of all levels might come into conflict with some higher authorities and the question will be over business, the discontent of authorities regarding inspections and financial claims. It is also possible that you will face the active opposition of your business partners. If you do get yourself into a complicated situation, try to be more diplomatic as things often tend to fall apart quickly. Mars, an aggressive and abrasive planet, has already been in your birth sign for two months and this means that you might overuse the pressure tactics and overdo the power games. It is also possible, however, that you are being worked over by people much more powerful and influential than yourself and for this reason, you need to be more flexible and not go shooting from the hip! The stars recommend not rushing events, especially concerning finances and liabilities. December will be a good month for you, but you are quite vulnerable at the moment. You should make a pause, stop and calm down.

Clerical workers are likely to have problems with a team of managers. In the worst-case scenario, you might be fired; if this is not a problem for you, go on as you are. If it is a problem for you, think twice before you act.
Money. Financially, October is quite a contradictory month. On the one

hand, you will keep receiving regular money as previously. On the other hand, your expenses will grow due to problems in either your working or your personal life.

Love and family. If major events have been happening in your personal life, the stars recommend toning things down. Try to remain neutral and not look for confrontation as you will gain little from any conflicts and they will certainly not help you to avoid any problems. Is your triumph worth the risk? Are you ready to split up? A step back is sometimes much more effective than banging your head against a brick wall.

It goes without saying that these recommendations are true for couples that have already had a number of problems in the past. If you have not, you will be able to avoid such situations, but you will need to support the person you love with tact, skill and patience as they might get themselves into a difficult situation.

Health. You are healthy this month but nervous and irritable; you need to stop sometimes and sleep well!

TAURUS

It seems that misfortunes of the recent past are now reaching their climax. If so, remember the old saying, 'The darkest hour comes before the dawn'; stand strong and take the punch!

Business. A difficult period continues where entrepreneurs and managers face another round of difficulties caused either by the authorities and their inspections or by some old legal problems.

Those who plan to move and start a business in a different city or abroad might fall under the wheels of justice and this will seriously jeopardize the development of your plan. You might even conclude that, no matter how hard you try, it is impossible - this does ring true given the present position of the planets. Later, however, towards the end of December, the planets move, and your position becomes more favorable. Hold on - a change for the better is coming.

Clerical workers will face problems at work. You need to be guarded towards your colleagues and not take sides in any plots or schemes; you may find yourself in a difficult situation and end up taking the fall.

Money. Money problems are quite possible given such a professional situation. Your income will fall while your expenses increase and unfortunately, this situation might turn out to be a long-lasting one. You should keep your financial documents in order and try to moderate your expenses; this advice is very important for the coming weeks.

Love and family. You will be less vulnerable in your personal life than in your professional life. Close relatives and friends will support you and back you up in even the thorniest of situations.

The situation with some of your relatives will worsen due to a major argument or other serious problems among your closest relatives. In both cases you might get help from your children or someone you love.

Health. Those who have happily avoided personal and professional problems might have problems with their health. You need to be alert to new disease or an acute episode of a chronic condition; see a good, experienced physician if necessary.

Drivers and those traveling should be extra cautious as the possibility of accidents and unpleasant situations on the road is really high in this difficult month; it would actually be better to cancel all trips.

GEMINI

A month of disappointment and uncompromising, bare-knuckle struggle lies ahead. When you find yourself in such an emotionally charged situation, the best thing you can do is to stop and take a deep breath.

Business. Those with whom you have been in conflict all summer might make further claims on you in October. The situation will be more complicated this time and your opponents' demands will be tougher and more uncompromising.

Former partners, old friends and high-ranking officials might act in a hostile manner over money or financial liabilities and it is possible that you will find these claims to be excessive. It seems impossible to reach a compromise at present and the situation seems deadlocked. You will only be able to sort out these highly charged matters in a few weeks, but for now, you will either have to pay out some money or start a real firefight - it is up to you to choose what you think best.

In addition, both managers and their employees need to be more attentive to those in the company who might start to play to their own tune. You might witness some unrest among the staff that interferes with business activities.

Money. The previous paragraph makes it clear that October might turn out to be ruinous and there is indeed the risk of serious loss, theft and other financial problems this month.

Financial professionals such as bank workers, brokers and accountants should be extra cautious.

Your personal expenses this month will be related to large purchases such as a flat, a house, interior decoration or home improvement. You are likely to receive the support of your parents, partner and close relatives in all financial matters this month.

Love and family. October might turn out to be quite a complicated period for lovers. There is nothing new, however, everything is a natural consequence of previous developments; you now have to dot the 'i's and cross the 't's, no matter how difficult it might be.
Families are facing comprehensive changes in their household and these might take up most of the family budget.

Health. Your energy levels are quite high this month but there is the possibility of accident, injury and other unpleasant events.

You should remember this and try to avoid dangerous situations if possible; perhaps by removing some events from your schedule.

CANCER

There might be times when it seems that peace is impossible and there is no path to victory - the position of the stars shows exactly this. Try to keep your head above water and remember that you are quite vulnerable at the moment.

Business. Confrontation with partners will seriously intensify and there will be attempts to sabotage your business or to break it up; this is actually the same thing. The position of your opponents is really strong, and it seems you have no means of countering them. The only thing that you can do at the moment is to involve some competent lawyers and just play for time. The situation will improve a little by the end of the year, however, and it will be easier for you to stand your ground then.

Clerical workers continue to face changes at work, and it may even come to the question of dismissal this month.

Your relationships with colleagues from other cities or overseas develop well and this is the only aspect of your activities that looks quite promising. In the case of serious problems, it might be wise to go somewhere, at least for the time being.

Money. The financial situation looks quite uncertain although your income and expenses are quite sensible and predictable.

Love and family. If your interests center on your personal life, you might find yourself in a rather unpleasant situation even here. The question on the agenda is a breakdown in relations and the situation might be really serious this time. The reason for the conflicts might be real estate or, worse, a joint business. Although the influence of relatives might smooth the situation over to some extent, it is unlikely to resolve it completely. You should be circumspect as the risk of being left with nothing is very high at the moment.

Health. Your energy levels are not high this month and your stressful environment might lead to serious health problems. In such a situation, the astrologer can only advise sleeping well and eating properly at regular times.

LEO

The odds might be against you this month. However, you are quite used to being stuck between a rock and a hard place and you will still manage to make progress.

Business. In October, many Leos will have to confront the same problems as have beset them for most of the summer; these might include complications in relationships with partners from other cities and overseas, legal questions or a long-running conflict with the authorities and their inspections. It is worth being guarded as some facts and events that you might have wished to remain secret could now come out into the open. This advice is true for all those of your sign who are professionally active, irrespective of their occupation.

Clerical workers will experience the prolonging of recent problems. All plans relating to faraway places might need to be reconsidered.

Despite all the trials and tribulations of October, you should try to keep your emotions in check, assess your capabilities clearly and try to take one step at a time. It is possible that all the logjam of misfortunes will remain without any hope of resolving it. This is regrettably the situation at the moment, but these troubles will pass in a few weeks.

Money. Despite a number of professional problems, the situation with money is satisfactory so far. You will receive regular inflows of cash and the approximate dates for receiving large amounts are the 3rd to the 5th, the 13th, 14th, the 21st to the 23rd, the 30th and the 31st of October.

Love and family. Those whose interests lie mainly in their personal lives will again have to confront a difficult situation with their relatives. If there has been an argument recently, it will not have abated yet. If some of your relatives have gotten themselves into a complicated situation or have fallen seriously ill, you will have to help them in word and in deed.

It is also possible that you will have to spend large amounts of money on helping your children.

Health. Those who have luckily escaped personal and professional troubles might have problems with their health. The elderly and those who have existing health problems should take care of themselves and take measures preventative of chronic illness. Drivers and those traveling should be extra cautious as the possibility of accidents and unpleasant situations is high this month. The astrologer recommends cancelling all journeys, especially long-distant ones, as they will only bring you problems.

VIRGO

Try to avoid error for this is a complicated month when your finances and relationships are under threat.

Business. It is possible that you will again be faced with a complicated situation related to finances and other liabilities in October. There is nothing new in this. It is more that the problem reaches its height and will require dealing with; this will turn out to be quite difficult as you have seemingly done nothing else but pay various bills for the last few weeks. Looking further ahead, we can say that this situation will extend out until nearly the end of the year and you will have to find various means of coping with it.

Relationships with partners from other cities and overseas will slow down for a time. Some of your colleagues might take their time making decisions whilst others just disappear into thin air, at least for a while. You might fall into a state of inertia and even start to doubt if you have chosen the right path. According to the stars, this is merely a rough patch and you should not jump to the wrong conclusions and become discouraged - the planets calm down in a few weeks and things will then get back into their groove.

Money. This month might turn out to be a difficult one financially. You will experience a regular drain of money due to your work or to your personal life and the needs of your family and children. Your income in October will be quite modest; you may even not earn anything at all.

Love and family. The situation in your personal life might be quite difficult. You are doing everything you can for your loved one to feel confident and comfortable and even if you have had an argument recently, you will be the first to take the steps towards making up.

You possibly will make up, but the question is for how long. Will the hoary old quarrels and demands resurface? It looks like that this is exactly what will happen. Still, if there is a chance of reconciliation you should undoubtedly take it and try to do everything in your power to stay together. If money problems impinge upon your relationship, you should either be generous to your partner or explain that things are tight at the moment and that you cannot.

All of this refers mainly to lovers. Married couples are likely, and not for the first time, to face serious expense related to their children; this is just how things are and you cannot really change the situation.

Health. Your energy levels are not high this month and there is a danger of injury. So, avoid dangerous situations and be careful while driving.

LIBRA

This month, you need to assess the situation, take stock and consider your opponent's capabilities. A long and serious fight lies ahead of you!

Business. You will step out of the shadows in October and test your mettle against partners and opponents who are serious-minded and will act quite rigidly and aggressively; indeed, they are prepared to cancel any negotiations in order to avoid compromise.

As fair play might not deliver any results, you may start saying one thing and doing another - this tactic will turn out to be the right one for as long as the playing field is not level.

That is why you should do what you think is right - you will succeed! If your partners leap into action, there is no reason why you shouldn't do just the same.

The problems remain the same – real estate, land or large property and

153

the astrologer has good grounds to think that the final result will be in your favor. However, you will still have to walk many miles and study lots of paperwork in order to withstand a real storm and all its unpleasantness.

Clerical workers will continue to fight with their rivals, and this is likely to continue for some time yet. You need to hold the fort but do not expect any support from managers and colleagues; at the moment you can only depend on your close friends, relatives and those you love.

Money. Despite all your professional troubles, you will not have any problems with money. You will experience a sufficient income of cash, even if there is some delay.

Love and family. If, by twist of fate, your interests center on your personal life, you will face some ongoing, long-term problems - you might even be so battle-weary, so fatigued by them that you consider them to be an inherent part of your life. Again, the issue might be either a house, a flat, a country house or other real estate that you have every right to consider as your property but that your partner, however, does not. So, most of October will be spent resolving these various claims and conflicts and this, of course, applies to couples who have already had a number of problems in the past.

With the help of their wisdom, patience and love, happy couples will cope with various domestic problems. There may be profound changes in your household, such as finishing a major refurbishment or finalizing the paperwork on some complicated real estate deal.

Health. Your energy levels are not high this month, but you should not worry about any serious illnesses.

SCORPIO

According to all the forecasts, October looks to be the most difficult month of the year. It seems as if all of your recent problems threaten to cancel out all of your recent achievements. You can, however, hold the line - you are the most stress-resistant sign of the zodiac!

Business. Entrepreneurs and managers of various levels will again be faced with old legal issues or with the tough requirements of the authorities and their inspections. This time you might find yourself at a dead end; it seems that your problems are endless and that you can hardly catch your breath. During this difficult period, you need to ask your friends or friendly highly placed officials for their help. You will get assistance this time and this will probably be like a life jacket for you. October is the most complicated time, but things become much easier as from November onwards.

Clerical workers might face discontent amongst staff members that causes problems for everyone. In the case of any machinations, you should not take sides as it would be easy to become the whipping boy.

Those who plan to move far away and start a business there will encounter complicated legislation and red tape that needs working on until the end of the year.

Money. The financial situation in October looks really uncertain; this is not surprising when everything around you is so difficult. You might expect a little money to arrive around the 20th of October.

Love and family. Many families will continue to experience the long-standing problems with their relatives that have been ongoing since the summer. Yet another unpleasant secret might be revealed this month causing the conflict to erupt again.

Those who are moving to faraway places might face immediate problems that turn out to be so serious that they either have to their change plans or to postpone them for a time. In such a situation, it is worth asking your friends for help as you really do need their support!

Health. October is not the best time regarding your health - a chronic condition might flare-up or a new illness appear. Drivers should remember that October is one of the most dangerous months of the year and the same can be said about travel to places both near and far. Indeed, if it is not urgent, you should cancel any trips entirely this month.

SAGITTARIUS

October is a month of tension and deadlock. Try to behave appropriately and try to avoid conflict!

Business. This month is a complex and contradictory one from a professional point of view and the main problem might turn out to be the complicated relationships with some of your friends, co-workers or high-ranking officials. This time, it will possibly be all about money or other such circumstances, reciprocal claims, unfulfilled promises or frustrated hopes.

Nevertheless, some of your affairs are developing well and this will positively affect your finances; something that you really need.

At the same time, managers should pay attention to their employees as not everything is as it should be personnel-wise. Clerical workers might face a similar situation and so they need to be guarded with their colleagues and not trust anyone with their secrets.

Money. The financial situation in October is not stable. The problem is not that there will be no income, but that your expenses will be extremely high. The astrologer sees most of these expenses as being related to your personal life; to the needs of your family, children and loved-one.

Love and family. The processes in your personal life that began in summer will continue. Many families are likely to have problems with their children; the lion's share of your family budget will be spent on the needs of the younger generation due to either the serious problems which they face or to your investment in their upbringing, education and development. It is possible that things simply seize up this month and it will be quite difficult to get going again.

October will be difficult for most lovers. Arguments happen one after another, and even though the thought might be hanging in the cold fall air, neither of you really knows whether you should split up or not.

All Sagittarians, regardless of their marital status, should note that this month, and especially in the second half of it, there might be quite a negative situation to face up to. You should be vigilant of rumour, gossip and intrigue and under no circumstances trust anybody with your secrets - you should listen rather than talk. In a month or six weeks, however, this state of affairs fades away.

Health. The second half of October will be difficult in respect of your health - you need to rest more, worry less and, in the most difficult moments, remember the wise words of King Solomon, 'this too shall pass'.

CAPRICORN

Your motto for this month is stability. When faced with obstacles, don't think about going around them or trying to force your way through them.

Business. There is a very active and very complicated period ahead of you. The problems which concerned you all summer will again demand your attention this month and will again concern real estate, land and other large property. Even if your position is a strong one and your opponents have to accept it as such, the skirmish is not yet over.

Looking further ahead, it is safe to say that you will definitely prevail, but at the cost of your time, strength and nerves. By acting steadily, step by step, you will be able to stand your ground and give your opponents no choice but to accept defeat and retreat accordingly, albeit slowly.

Your relations with colleagues from other cities and overseas develop well and you might have a successful journey this month.

Relations with certain people become more complicated during the second half of October. Friends, co-workers or some high-ranking officials might become duplicitous and not fulfil the obligations which they had earlier undertaken; this is not so grave at the moment because you are prepared to stand alone.

Money. From a financial point of view, this month is not bad. You will receive regular inflows of cash and the amount will increase to some extent. There will be many expenses, most of which are related to your current difficulties.

Love and family. The central events of this month will possibly happen in your home, within your family.

You cannot hope for much harmony as the sector of the sky responsible for peace and tranquillity in the family is occupied by the aggressive Mars. Couples who have had previous problems will understand this very well; conflict will become a regular occurrence and all the most worrying questions revolve around residential property or other disputed real estate. In the most difficult cases, you will start to discuss divorce and the situation is really serious this time - breaking up is more than likely.

The situation looks a little bit better for lovers; you might go on a journey together and this will improve your relationship and help you to start thinking about the future.

The stars recommend all lovers born under this sign not to trust friends and not to allow them to interfere in your personal matters; they might hurt your partner either by accident or out of malice and this will result in conflict.

Health. Your energy levels are quite high this month and there is nothing health-wise to worry about except for some nervous strain.

AQUARIUS

You really want to move forward this month, but the circumstances actually warrant stopping. Even if you do have to take a step back, remember that your goals are achievable!

Business. Many Aquarians will again face problems arising from the past in October. These may be either complicated relationships with your colleagues from other cities or overseas or legal problems. The situation looks more demanding this time and it seems that you are at a stalemate. The problems will, in fact, linger on but one cannot say that they are unmanageable. The sky will clear in a couple of months, so don't give up but keep addressing your current issues one by one. You should always bear in mind the old words of wisdom, still true today, 'A journey of a thousand miles begins with a single step'.

The stars also recommend being attentive to those around you. It is possible that your enemies, both overt and covert, will become especially active. They will be up to no good and try to discover some of your secrets; you should stand fast and not give such venomous people any reason to gossip and spread conspiracies.

Clerical workers will be faced with changes at work, but the astrologer has good reason to believe that they will lead to benefits rather than drawbacks.

Money. The financial situation is stable this month and it seems that your professional problems do not affect your finances – this is a good thing. Your income and expenses in October are sensible and predictable.

Love and family. In your personal life, events originating in the past will further develop. The main issue is that problems with relatives are not only remain unsolved but appear to be heating up. The circumstances might appear different; there might be a serious, long-term argument or troubles that have been visited upon one of your family members.

The situation for lovers will be no better. Some malicious actors might interfere in their relationship and reveal things they wished to remain secret. Married couples will continue to improve their home and this process seems to be reaching its end.

Health. Your energy levels are not high this month. Those suffering from migraines or chronic heart disease or those generally under the weather will be at risk.

Drivers and those traveling should be extra cautious this month as the danger of accidents is very high. It is better to cancel all trips this month as they might not go the way you had planned and dreamed.

pisces

You are facing one of the most difficult periods of the year. Things and people who had seemed to be of utmost impor-

tance to you not so long ago will become irrelevant.

Business. This month you will again have to deal with a number of problems that began in the summer. They entail financial disagreements with former friends or highly placed patrons and the question is possibly over debt obligations or possibly moral issues; the situation looks to be at an impasse as none of the parties are ready to make concessions. As you are unable to change anything this month, you should take a step back and decide what you want and what you expect from the future.

You have some time – six weeks to two months – in which to make your final decision. You should also involve any allies you have since you will reinforce your position by doing so.

Your relationships with colleagues from other cities or overseas are developing well and this area of your life looks quite positive.

Trips that you planned for October might be successful.

Money. The financial situation looks quite tense. You will experience regular leaks of money related to either your professional sphere or to your personal life.

Love and family. Your personal life might be really unstable, if not stressful, this month. The future of couples in trouble looks vague and obscure; there are many questions but no answers at the moment. The stars recommend being gentle instead of pushy - try to compromise on the problems, no matter how difficult it might seem at times.

If it comes to divorce, spouses might become embroiled in the division of property and disputes over their children's future.

Health. Those who are not concerned about personal and professional matters might have problems with their health.

You should not strength test your body with excessive behavior in October. If you cannot avoid stressful situations, at least try to sleep well.

You should also avoid risky situations as the possibility of misfortune is quite high this month.

NOVEMBER

ARIES

You have been working really hard recently - fighting for your place in the sun. All of your efforts will soon bear fruit!

Business. The complicated situation that has been preying on you for a long time seems to be subsiding. It's still too early to talk about a total solution but the last twenty days of the month will prove that it is not only you, but also your opponents, who are exhausted by the fight. It therefore looks like now is the time to consider a possible compromise and all opposing parties will realise this towards the end of November. Misunderstandings and hissy fits are still possible, but this will be nothing compared to the summer or to last month.

Financial issues are likely to emerge during the current period and there might initially be some bargaining followed by compromises from both sides; some questions will be sorted out more informally. There are likely to be backroom deals and the assistance of allies - in this way, with joint efforts, you will be able to achieve a compromise. It will possibly happen closer to New Year but at the moment you are doing extensive work preparing peace initiatives.

Clerical workers might consider the possibility of a new job and the circumstances are favorable here as some of your old friends will offer you a new job in the very near future. During November you will be busy reflecting, sorting out papers and other matters and finishing up old tasks. There might be constant conflict with the authorities but, oddly enough, it is you who initiates it.

Money. Although it is difficult to describe your financial situation in November as stable, nothing disastrous is going to happen. You will have both income and expenses; your balance will still be positive at the end of the month. For those whose activities concern finance, the stars recommend controlling the situation, avoiding risk and thinking several moves ahead - this will protect you from losses both now and in the future.

Love and family. As long as Mars remains in your sign, you might be excessively demanding and harsh in your personal relationships and this causes conflict with your partner, who is the more diplomatic one at this time.

From the star's point of view, you should listen to your loved one as they are more rational about the current situation and tend towards mutual compromise. This advice is true both for happily married couples and for those who are on the verge of breaking up or divorcing.

In this case, it is your partner who might offer the best proposal for the division of any property and this would be well worth looking into.

Health. Your energy levels are not high in November, so take better care of yourself and try to keep away from the typical fall infections. Should you have any chronic diseases, you need to take preventative measures.

TAURUS

The skies above you will slowly start to clear this month.
Even if the problem still persists, there is light at the end of
the tunnel.

Business. From a professional point of view, November might be quite unpredictable. On the one hand the problems of the last few months are still pending but on the other hand you will find some allies and co-workers and with their help the situation will settle down and become more manageable. The problems may relate to aged legal issues or to complications with moving to a different city or abroad and starting a business there.

In any case, the stars recommend being cautious and flexible in your problem solving and taking advantage of any new opportunities - even if they seem difficult to integrate at times.

In addition, entrepreneurs and managers will continue to have complications in their relationships with their employees, and clerical workers with their colleagues. You have to deal with maneuvers, disagreements and discontent among the staff.

Money. This month is really difficult financially. Your income will fall whilst your expenses rise. This negative trend will unfortunately also continue into next month.

Love and family. You might be faced with the same problems in your personal life as in previous months. Your relationships with your relatives are still complicated but here you can rely on support from your spouse or partner; they act as a mediator and protector and their participation in family matters turns out to be both positive and useful. This true for both situations caused by family arguments and for other problems with close relatives.

Those moving faraway will, with some difficulty, solve a number of their complicated recent issues.

Health. Your energy levels are not high this month and the stars further recommend being careful while driving and traveling as the possibility of accident and injury remains high.

GEMINI

On the one hand the chances of both doing and achieving a lot are good this month. On the other hand, you will have to sacrifice your routine in order to succeed.

Business. You will have plenty to do in November and many of your initiatives that were previously deadlocked will proceed. Entrepreneurs and managers of all levels might expect support from their employees who will be active and well-organised this time.

Relationships with the authorities will improve for those clerical workers who have earned it with their hard work.

Nevertheless, recently arisen problems will continue; these might be old financial disagreements with friends, former co-workers or some high-ranking officials. Although some of the issues are being solved and the conflicts seem to fade away, they could flare up later on. The situation is improving but it might take time and not work out exactly as you had hoped. You will, however, be able to extricate yourself step by step.

Money. The financial situation looks more positive in November when compared to previous months. You will have regular inflows of cash and the approximate dates for the arrival of large sums are the 5th, 6th, 14th, 15th and the 22nd to the 24th of November. In addition to your regular earnings, you might count on loans and the financial support of your friends and close relatives. This will allow you to pay off your debts and to partially resolve any recent financial disputes.

Love and family. Even if you notice some improvements at work, they are unlikely to be replicated in your personal life this month.

The disagreements of the previous months over finances, differing views on life and value systems continue for lovers; indeed, the situation is approaching its end game and the outcome is unlikely to be positive.

Families might have difficulties with children and could face major expenses related to their children's problems.

Health. Many Gemini will feel not quite so confident and active in November. You should be alert to your health and especially so if you have already had some issues with it. People with migraines, chronic heart disease or the threat of stroke should take extra care; the possibility of suffering an acute episode of a chronic disease is quite high this month.

Young and healthy people should give up or cut down on habits detrimental to their health and adopt a healthier way of life. This is a good month for face and body treatments, visiting a spa or health resort and other recreational activities.

CANCER

November will be stressful and turbulent. Any emotional outbursts in the middle of the month need to be controlled; otherwise you will be left celebrating your successes on your own.

Business. The problems of recent months are still a priority and again the question is over disagreements with partners or over the division of a joint business. Although none of this is new to you, the situation will improve somewhat this month with the help of lawyers, friends, old friends or close relatives who act as mediators.

Your relationship with colleagues from faraway will be noticeably revitalized and you might have a successful journey.

Nevertheless, the problem with some high-ranking officials might continue and it is unlikely that you will be able to completely resolve it in the near future; December looks much better in this respect and so it makes sense to wait.

Clerical workers are likely to face some major changes at work that will only be completely settled next month - there is no point in trying to change anything at the moment or addressing management with any requests. During this quite complicated month you should not pressure people too much but try to make your point in a less obtrusive manner as only then will you be heard and understood.

Money. November does not look very promising financially. Your expenses will increase due to work or to problems in your personal life.

Love and family. Complications in your family life drag on and again the reason is joint property - more than likely residential. However, the situation will improve in November and this time children might be the mediators; their influence on your partner will soften any hostile sentiment and allow you to revisit some disputed issues.

Lovers might go on a journey together that refreshes and improves their relationship.

Happy couples will spend lots of time with their children and this will make them happy.

Health. Your energy levels are quite high this month and you should not worry about your health. November is an excellent time to go to the theatre or a museum, to travel a long or short distance or just to have a stroll outside.

LEO

Despite your sociable nature, you should limit contact with others in November. You will work better and enjoy your holiday more either alone or in the company of only your closest friends or relatives.

Business. From a professional point of view, November is not very auspicious. The best thing you can do at the moment is to analyse the situations that have been disquieting you over the last few months and to try to find the best possible way out. The problems of the recent past are still pending; whether caused by the controlling authorities and their inspections or by old legal problems.

If you have ties with colleagues from other cities or overseas, you might once again come up against their unpredictable nature or, at times, even their hostile attitude. This requires thorough consideration and good preparation and November is a perfect opportunity for this as you will receive support from close friends, relatives and family members.

Money. The financial situation in November can best be described as neutral. You will not be without money, but most of it will come from your close friends, parents, relatives or spouse. A little money will come in from real estate deals and from interest on bank accounts.

Love and family. Personal and family matters might be your priority this month. Those with family will put their house in order and spend a lot of time with their close friends and relatives.

Your relationships with your relatives are still not yet perfect; conflicts continue but the situation will become more manageable and peaceful due to the involvement of some senior family members. This is also true if some of your relatives have recently had some kind of problem.

Health. Your energy levels are not high this month, so take care of yourself and keep to your limits. Drivers and those traveling still need to be more cautious as the possibility of accident is still high in November!

VIRGO

You are extremely active and restless this month. These qualities will help you to solve many problems at work and in love.

Business. From a professional point of view, this is a very productive and positive period. Your relationships with colleagues from other cities and overseas will develop and you will possibly go on a successful trip which helps you to either resolve or partly smooth over a few recent problems. Again, the question is over finances and other pending liabilities; this causes plenty of stress.
November is a good time for important meetings and negotiations and the most productive time is the second half of the month. In any situation you should try to clearly explain your point of view to others in a diplomatic fashion.

Money. Despite the improved professional situation, there are still money problems. They are regular leaks of money as a result of your debts or the needs of your family, children and close circle of friends. In any case you need to be careful when spending money because the astrologer notices that your expenditure seems excessive.

Love and family. The processes in your personal life that arose over the summer continue. People with family are still concerned about their children's problems and will invest large sums into their future. In a different scenario, you will have to solve your children's problems and expend not only your money but your efforts and nerves on them.

Your relationships with your relatives become more active and you might go on a trip with them or meet those living in a different city or abroad.

Relations between lovers are still not perfect. Despite frequent arguments, the intensity of your emotions fades away. Those who can survive this might stay together but those who are less strong might finally think of breaking up, and, according to the astrologer, this might not be such a bad thing - there are plenty more fish in the sea.

Health. Your energy levels are quite high this month and there is no need to worry about your health. Nevertheless, the stars recommend avoiding physically risky situations and being more careful while driving. Mars is in an unfavourable sector of your sky and it might cause a number of unexpected problems.

LIBRA

There is another month of anxiety and instability ahead of you. You might sense the heavy hand of time and rush unnecessarily. Stop! You need total concentration and rock-solid self-assurance now - more than ever before.

Business. The complicated period in your professional life continues. There will be moments when winning appears impossible and this does seem to be true given the position of the stars in November. Nevertheless, the situation is temporary and your goal at the moment is simply not to lose any ground.

The position of the stars changes in December and you will find yourself in a more advantageous position. So, hold the fort and counteract the aggressive, pushy attitude of your opponents with flexibility and confident diplomacy. It is possible that money turns out to be a promising approach in helping you to partially resolve disputes over real estate, land or large property.

However, you still need to exercise caution as your more treacherous opponents might have a nasty surprise up their sleeves for you. For this reason, you should keep some of your powder dry, at least for now.

Money. November is quite a favourable one financially as you will experience regular and increasing inflows of money.

The approximate dates in November for larger amounts to arrive in your account are the 5th, 6th, 14th, 15th, 22nd and 23rd.

There will be expenses that naturally relate to both personal and professional problems; some of the problems might, however, be quite unexpected.

Love and family. You will need to again be unflappable in your personal life as your patience is the best answer to the aggressive attitude of your partner. In the case of divorce, you will try to solve the problem of severance peacefully, but your suggestions will be taken as weakness and your partner will try to pressure you further. All financial offers might have either a very weak or a short-term effect; indeed, some offers will be flatly rejected and your partner will demand yet more.

Happily married couples will still be busy resolving important questions related to land or real estate and will slowly but surely deal with a number of problems that could spring up in the future.

Health. As your energy levels are not so high this month, you need to keep proper hours and exercise in the mornings in order to keep yourself away from the colds and infections of the fall.

SCORPIO

This month brings success in business matters that had earlier seemed hopeless and which many people had refused to deal with. Good luck!

Business. This month you will bite the bullet and finally get things under control - it is fair to say that you will succeed in many situations.

This month entrepreneurs and those who plan to co-operate with colleagues from other cities or overseas will see the peaceful resolution of recent problems. Even if some things do not go entirely smoothly and there is still the occasional hissy fit, improvements are noticeable. The astrologer assumes that these improvements are mainly your own accomplishments. The same can be said about those who have worked at their legal problems doggedly and courageously and have managed to limit the number of inspections from various authorities. Some disputes will be sorted out in the second half of November and the rest next month.

Trips that you planned for the second half of November will turn out to be really successful.

Money. The financial situation will improve towards the end of the month and you might receive a substantial amount of money in your account between the 25th and the 28th of November. You will not have many expenses; most of them relate to difficult recent situations.

Love and family. You may also notice some improvement in your personal life. The situation with your relatives is becoming quieter and it is you who has been making the effort to harmonize the relationships. This is true for both recent, prolonged conflicts and for problems into which your relatives have accidentally gotten themselves. Those moving far away will have to overcome a number of complicated issues related to regulations and other legal technicalities.

Your relationships with your children will improve and they are probably the ones who have helped you resolve many recent problems.

It is a good time in the love department. Lovers separated by time and distance will be reunited. The best time to deal with personal situations is in the second half of November.

Health. Your energy levels will improve noticeably this month and even those who fell ill last month will quickly recover. The situation on the roads still does not look good this month, however, and the stars beg you to be more careful whilst driving.

SAGITTARIUS

You do not always have to advance by yourself - if you reach for support, it will be there. The old saying, 'No man is an island' is true for you now as never before.

Business. You have lately been beavering away on your own in an attempt to solve various problems, but the time has now come to take the arm of old friends, a partner or those close to you; the circumstances will eventually start to develop positively for you. This process might not seem so obvious in November as old financial difficulties or problems with opponents or high-ranking officials remain evident, but the situation is improving nevertheless, and this will become much more noticeable one way or another next month.

There is one more piece of advice – November is a good time for some undercover campaigns. You will gain more from these as overt maneuverings are not as effective at the moment and will do you no good. Even if you are set in your ways of acting, you should take a different path once in a while.

Money. The financial situation will improve significantly due to the financial support of favorably disposed partners or someone close to you. There might also be earnings from various real estate deals, loans or lines of credit.

Love and family. The situation in your personal life remains complicated. Problems with your children continue and the lion's share of your family budget will again go towards paying for their needs. You will receive help this month in both word and deed from your spouse, parents or others close to you.

This month will be a problematic one for most lovers. If your feelings for each other are still alive, you will merely face misunderstandings and arguments. If, however, your feelings for each other are over, you will have to endure a painful period of loneliness. If this should come to pass, you need to maintain an emotional balance and remember that the world is a big place and that your soulmate is out there somewhere.

Health. Your energy levels are not high this month, and you might be at risk of various infections and colds.

The most difficult days in this respect will be during the new moon of the 14th to the 15th of November. Try to spend them quietly, as the next Moon phase will then pass without any problems.

CAPRICORN

The dark skies begin to brighten up this month. Even if the situation still looks somewhat bleak and capricious, it is better than nothing, however. Besides, this is only the start!

Business. Professionally active Capricorns will be able to resolve a number of their past problems over real estate or a joint business this month. It is possible that people ready to help you - either old friends or high-ranking officials - will appear over the horizon.

Thanks to their help, and with your own efforts, your business will enter the home stretch in the second ten days of the month and you will cross the finishing line sometime in December.

Your relationships with colleagues from other cities or overseas are developing well and there might be a successful journey ahead.

This month is also a good one for clerical workers - even if there are changes afoot in their company, there are only gains to be made from them.

Money. Despite the number of professional problems, there will be no financial difficulties. You will have regular and increasing inflows of money.

At the same time, however, your expenses will also increase; they will be related either directly to your business or to family problems.

Love and family. You will keep treading the same old boards in your personal life. In some cases, you will eventually have to admit to yourself that you cannot step into the same river twice and that some things should be left in the past where they belong. This is mostly true for couples who still have unresolved issues over money, family valuables or real estate.

You are likely to have some problems with your children; the situations will differ for each family and depend on recent events.
This month is also a complicated one for lovers. There might be unexpected arguments that push your relationship to the brink. Don't jump to conclusions, however, as the alignment of the stars changes in December and you will find yourself in a more favorable position; the same could indeed be said of your partner. At the moment you need to stop, take a deep breath and calm yourself down.

Health. You are really active, sociable and healthy this month; it means that health problems are not a concern.

AQUARIUS

You have been working hard recently and you can now see your goal ahead of you. This month and those ahead are good for taking action. So, don't sit back and do nothing but square up to any difficulties.

Business. You will be at your peak in November and able to move mountains, or at least to solve the problems of recent months much more easily. This is true for both those who have been dealing with the authorities and their inspections and those who have been trying to sort out various legal questions.

Relationships with colleagues from other cities or overseas are developing with varying degrees of success. You still have problems, but towards the end of November it will become clear that they are all quite manageable. Indeed, most of the complicated issues which have been worrying you recently will be sorted out one way or another in December.

Money. The financial situation looks good this month with regular inflows of money in increased amounts. The approximate dates for the receipt of large sums of money are the 5th, 6th, 14th, 15th, and the 22nd to the 24th of November.

Love and family. Your personal life is less important to you than work this month. Nevertheless, those whose life is centered on love and family will face the same old problems again this month. Your relationships with your relatives remain tricky and there might well be fiery outbursts due to pernicious disagreements or to the frustratingly endless troubles of someone close to you.

Those moving faraway will continue to deal with various problems and will succeed with many of them in November.

Lovers might feel uncomfortable in November. The past few months have revealed many things to you and the problems you once managed to side-step now demand your serious attention. You might have to make a decision that is unlikely to be a positive one; if your fortune should point you in a different direction, it will only be for the better.

Health. You are healthy, active and ready to move mountains in November and without a shadow of doubt, these qualities are very necessary at the moment.

pisces

November is not bad in general. It may be, however, that you are merely drifting in the white water that is your life and so you need to put your back into it if you want to get to the right place at the right time.

Business. There is an excellent opportunity for you to sort out some recent problems this month. These are primarily financial disagreements with some of your friends or high-ranking officials and you might receive decent legal assistance or support from your colleagues from other cities or overseas this month. Thanks to this, some of these complicated and disputed issues will be resolved in the second half of November with the rest next month. The problems are so serious that there might be even outbreaks of previous hostilities during this more positive period. Time is on your side, however.

Journeys planned for November will generally be successful ones that might bring constructive negotiations and additional profit.

Money. The financial situation will improve but you can hardly call it stable. You will constantly leak money as a result of dealing with recent problems; either professional or of a personal and family nature.

Love and family. The situation in your personal life is still complicated and it will be almost impossible to resolve. Again, the relationships between lovers and unhappily married couples are under threat. The core of the problem for lovers might be moral or financial whereas for couples on the verge of divorce, it might be material values.

The influence of some relatives might reduce the tension between the parties and the situation will ease in the second ten days of November. December will be positive in all respects and you will then be able to solve many disputed questions and, as the astrologer sees it, to get your own back - if not totally, at least in part. This is quite a good and necessary trade off.

Happily married couples might go on a journey that lowers the general tension stemming from situations that either spouse might have had at work.

Health. Your energy levels will increase this month and even those who fell ill last month will recover quickly. Drivers are recommended to be extra careful on the roads this month as the possibility of accidents and unpleasant situations is still fairly high.

DECEMBER

ARIES

The time has come for you to move on and to stop dredging up the past. The situation is changing to your advantage and many achievements now lie ahead of you. Good luck to you - the zodiac's most active sign!

Business. The complicated problems of previous months have eventually been resolved and you will now have the chance to work to a quieter schedule. Your relationships with colleagues from other cities or overseas become important and negotiations happen as part of the everyday course of business; without any haste or stress. You are likely to go on a journey that opens new doors - new opportunities and prospects. In addition, new and influential people and patrons appear on your horizon.

Many of your birth sign will renew old friendships that favorably affect your business. The only warning from the stars is to be attentive and cautious when signing any agreements or important financial documents. You will need to consider things carefully and attempt to foresee all possible variants including the not so favourable and any force-majeure situations. The future will prove that these precautions were the right thing to do since they will save you from many misfortunes in 2021.

Money. The financial situation is stable in December. You will have regular inflows of money and the amounts will increase somewhat. The largest sum will arrive at the end of the month between the 24th and the 27th of December.

Love and family. There are many positive changes in your personal life. Mainly, you will stop being so anxious and fussy and this will immediately improve your relationships with those you love. You might go on a trip together and meet relatives, old friends and new people.

Complex situations regarding ownership or a joint business will be successfully resolved and mean either the conclusion of long-lasting disagreements over divorce or a joint solution to situations in which your spouse or family have found themselves.

Single people might go on a journey and have a steamy love affair. Indeed, the possibility of meeting new people and having a fling this month is quite high so don't miss out on any parties and do not forget to dress up.

Health. Your energy levels are quite high this month, and this will be especially noticeable after the new moon on the 14th of December.

You will celebrate the New Year in the company of people you love in an atmosphere that is bright, merry and exciting.

TAURUS

For the first time in a long time you can take a breather. All the storms are behind you and now is the time to figure out what happened and to put your affairs, thoughts and feelings in order.

Business. A new, active and positive period is soon to begin in your professional life and at the moment you need to deal with all the various organizational activities that are prerequisites to your next breakthrough. The complicated and contentious issues that have recently dogged you seem to have ended. Although some misunderstandings are still possible on or about the 20th of December, they pale in comparison with the events of the summer and fall of this year. This is true for all professionally active Taureans, regardless of their occupation.

Those eager to move far away and start a business there will see their dreams come true in the coming year. Those who have had some problems with colleagues from other cities or overseas are very close to achieving a complete resolution; at the very least, the main battles are now over. The same can be said for those who have been fighting with the authorities and their inspections or who have been sorting out a thorny legal issue. Even if you have lost a little you should not worry about it too much – there are lots of good things in front of you!

Money. December is financially stable but nothing more. You will not have a lot of earnings and most of your income comes from loans, interest on your bank accounts and help from business partners, close friends or relatives. Your expenses in December will be related to friends or those who have previously helped you through difficult times.

Love and family. The difficulties in your personal life also ease off. Long standing problems with your relatives have been successfully resolved either due to the conclusion of an old argument or to the end of some convoluted situation concerning some of your relatives.

People moving faraway will successfully cope with all the difficulties thrown up by this complicated process.

December is a perfect time for sorting out all household matters and celebrating the happiest of holidays.

You are likely to celebrate the New Year either far from home or amongst those you love; among your friends and relatives

Health. Your energy levels are not high this month, but you are unlikely to fall ill. A healthy way of life and a good night's sleep will help you cope with any weakness or tiredness. You should be careful while driving on or about the 20th of December.

GEMINI

A significant and stressful chapter in your life has closed for the better and the long, open road to the future lies ahead.

Business.
This month sees an end to the long-lasting lawsuit over which you have

lately lost sleep. You will find allies in December who act as mediators and who can resolve the most heavily disputed issues you have had with your unfriendly and hostile opponents. In this respect, the second half of December is of more consequence when serious planets such as Jupiter and Saturn not only help eliminate recent problems but also help illuminate the path to a better future.

Many Gemini have plans to move to a new house either in a different city or abroad. These plans will be fulfilled at different times over the coming year, but you can make preparations now and discuss how you will turn the plan into reality.

Money. December is quite neutral financially. Your earnings and your expenses are moderate although you will have to pay out a large sum of money on or about the 20th of December.

Love and family. Everything is quiet in your personal life; either due to the end of an unhealthy and toxic relationship or to having made up with your partner - the astrologer sees the former as being the more realistic. With the exception of those happily married for some time, unstable married couples are unlikely to cope with the pressure of the planets.

This month, many of your sign will start to think about moving to a new place, although for some this means returning to places where they have already lived or often visited.

Health. Your energy levels are not high this month and there is a strong possibility of accident and injury on or about the 20th of December - remember this and be careful.
You might spend the New Year among people close to you professionally and the stars recommend not eating or drinking to excess as there may be consequences.

CANCER

You have a good chance to improve your financial and professional standing in December. The transition of Jupiter and Saturn allows you to draw a line under the problems that ended all your previous hopes.

Business. This month is a good one professionally and, by fixing old problems with opponents, you will be able to bring about a bright and positive change to your business.

Legal questions that have been poisoning your life for a long time will be sorted out this month. Although things may not develop in quite the way in which you had planned or dreamed, the story is not yet finished - this is a positive. You will have the chance to worry not about the past but about future business and future work. As the changes are unlikely to happen all at once, however, you will at least have the time to consider and to plan your actions.

Clerical workers will acquit themselves well, but the idea of changing jobs is still in the air and it is certain to happen in the near future.

Money. The financial situation improves to some extent, but you cannot yet call it stable - you need to be thrifty and think everything over a few times before investing any money.

Love and family. Everything becomes quiet in your personal life. This is especially true for spouses going through a divorce and those now set on a divorce settlement; it is a time for licking your wounds and totaling your gains and losses. There is a long year ahead when you will have to get used to living in an unfamiliar way or to being single. If you do find yourself in such a difficult and uncomfortable situation, do not be upset because after 2021 has finished you will come to a new period of your life that is brighter; more exciting and more positive. So, you have time to put your affairs, thoughts and feelings in order.

Happily married couples will start to consider moving to a new place; be it a new flat or a new house and this might well come to pass at some point in 2021.

Children make you happy and might even become the bridge between hostile spouses in families with problems.

Health. Your energy levels are not high this month so take good care of yourself and keep everything within its limits.

LEO

One of the most exciting months of the year lies ahead as problems vanish and co-operation at work and in love await you.

Business. You will finally be able to draw a line under the most difficult questions that have bothered you for a while and not allowed you sleep or even rest. These were the complicated relationships with distant colleagues, the authorities and their inspections and legal issues; all can now be left behind, and you are on the verge of a better and more positive period in your life. Influential partners will appear on the horizon in the second half of the month and they might even turn out to be already known to you.

The stars forecast a renewal of relationships with some of your former colleagues. Despite an excellent beginning, you should be cautious when signing important documents about co-operation and take into account all complications possible in 2021.

Clerical workers will start to think about changing jobs and they will fulfil these plans towards the end of December or in January 2021.

Money. December seems financially unstable to the astrologer as you will face extra expense related mainly to your personal life and family needs.

Love and family. This month is not bad for your personal life. Those with family will spend lots of time with their children and this will make everybody happy.

Complicated relationships with relatives will be put right in one way or another and family relationships will become much better and warmer as a result.

Single people and those disappointed by former relationships might unexpectedly fall in love in the second half of the month and their new lover will somehow be connected to their past.

You might go on a journey which will be really successful.

Health. You are full of energy and very attractive this month. The stars do warn you, however, not to eat or drink to excess during the New Year celebrations as your state of health might suffer.

VIRGO

The events of recent months could have shattered your belief in a better future. However, the situation takes on a new twist this month as your run of bad luck ends and ahead of you lies work and money - everything you have been trying to achieve for such a long time.

Business. As from the middle of December, all professionally active Virgos will come upon surprising new opportunities and you will need to utterly devote yourself to them; there will be different work to do but you are completely ready for it. The problems of past months are vanishing, but there are, however, new ones already looming on the horizon. Although there are no immediate problems, the astrologer predicts, when looking further ahead, that one of the main complications in 2021 will be your relationships with colleagues from other cities or overseas. This is why you need to be very cautious when signing documents and try to cover all the bases; including the negative and the force-majeure. By doing so, you will save yourself from the misfortunes which might possibly happen in the first half of 2021.

Clerical workers might expect new job offers from someone they know from a previous place of work.

Money. The financially situation trends to the better and this will become noticeable in the second half of the month. The key point is that this favorable situation will continue into 2021.

Love and family. There are many changes in your personal life and most of them are promising ones. Many families have come together to deal with their recent problems and your close relatives are now ready to help you. Some changes at home, such as repairs or purchasing furniture and decorative items are likely. Old problems related to children will be successfully sorted out although a final payment is due about the 20th of December.

It is difficult to say anything about lovers, but it is quite possible that they did not survive the pressure of the stars and broke up not so long ago.

Health. Your energy levels are not high this month and you will encounter a period in the near future when you have to be very careful with your body. In order to avoid problems in the near future, the stars recommend re-assessing your habits; giving up unhealthy lifestyle choices and taking up healthy ones.

LIBRA

You seem to have achieved the goal for which you were well-set. There are some outstanding details, but you will deal with them successfully in December. 2021 opens new doors for you and brings you new partners to work with.

Business. You will enter a more serene and predictable period in your life. Conflict with toxic opponents is left behind thanks to the incredible efforts of favourably disposed mediators, friends and close relatives who made it possible to placate the opposing party and open a new chapter in your career. As a result, the things which you consider yours will remain yours; you do not need what is not.

The serious problem this month will be your relationships with some who were supposed to help you. For entrepreneurs and managers these will be their employees and for clerical workers, their colleagues.

This needs to be kept under tight control as you will have to deal variously with the laziness, dishonesty, indifference or incompetence that interferes with your work not only now, but also in the near future.

Money. The financial situation is stable; you will have a regular inflow of money and the amount will increase noticeably. The approximate dates for receiving large sums of money are the 2nd to the 4th, the 11th, 12th, 20th, 21st and the 29th to the31st of December. You will not have many expenses, but this is only a temporary situation as you can expect to make lots of investments in your business and needs of the people you love in

2021.

Love and family. Those whose interests center on their personal lives and whose problems have been connected to close friends and relatives for a long time will be able to breathe more easily. Any conflicts related to the partition of property - mainly of the flat or house - will finish.

The most important thing is your relationship with your children. It seems that after some long-term doubts, they will take your side and you will then take responsibility for them for some time to come.

All of this is true for divorced couples or spouses going through a divorce. Happily married couples will deal with recent problems together and will take care of their children's future.

Single people have interesting and exciting events ahead of them. Old acquaintances will appear over the horizon in the second half of December and there might be an unexpected affair.

Health. Your energy levels are quite high this month and you should not worry about your health. You will celebrate the New Year with those close to you professionally; it will be a very exciting and positive occasion.

SCORPIO

You will find the energy and resources this month to forever
break free of the problems of the past. Good luck!

Business. You eventually enter a favorable and predictable period professionally. Any problems with partners from other cities or overseas will recede. If there are, however, any problems with the authorities and their inspections, you will have to find ways of resolving the most disputed and complex issues.

Those who plan to start a business in a different city or abroad will start working on their real estate solutions in the second half of the month. At various points in 2021, they will succeed in patching things up regarding the business processes.

Nevertheless, despite the obvious improvement in the situation, you should be careful and vigilant. You will have to face up to some aggression in the first months of 2021, but you will be better able to cope with it than it you have been recently.

Money. This month is a positive one financially. You will have regular inflows of money and the significant increase in the amount gives you the chance to pay off your debts and solve the knottiest issues that have been bothering you recently.

Love and family. Times of change in your personal life have arrived. Many Scorpions will find new accommodation in the second part of the month; this is true both for those moving far away and for those who staying closer to home.
The complicated relationships with your relatives are nearly sorted as the old arguments run aground and the old issues of your family members are put to rights.

A final outbreak of misfortune is possible around the 20th of December but after that there will be an extended period of peace and quiet in your family.

Health. Your energy levels are quite high this month, but you should be extra careful while traveling and driving between the 20th and the 25th of December.

You might spend the New Year visiting or welcoming friends from faraway.

SAGITTARIUS

It is very important not to spread yourself too thin, but to gather your wits about you and achieve more at a lower cost. You are at a turning point, so you need to set yourself specific goals and then put them into action!

Business. This month your patron, the powerful Jupiter - with the support of another powerful planet Saturn - is transitioning. This means that many things that bothered you in the past disappear, and you will see new possibilities ahead.

Many Sagittarians will start to consider a move to a different city or abroad and will make these plans reality at different times in 2021. It is possible that some very promising co-operation develops with colleagues from other cities or overseas and that you establish a business far away from your home. It is also possible that you renew old ties or return to a place you have visited many times before.

To those who plan to start a new business, the stars advise building a team as its absence might be the only thing to disrupt your plans for 2021.

Money. The financial situation will significantly improve this month and this becomes more noticeable towards the end of December. Your expenses will fall and this is directly related to the end of the problems that have recently bothered you. Some money will need to be paid out about the 20th of December in respect of a debt from the past.

Love and family. The situation in your personal life will stabilize. In particular, misunderstandings with children and the related expenses will come to an end. This is true for both those couples who have differing views on the upbringing and future of their children and for those couples going through a divorce and trying to retain some influence over their offspring.

In a different scenario, your children's problems will finish; you will be able to draw a line under these problems in December.

Lovers who managed to get through difficult times will be able to come to mutual agreement this month - to breakup or to get back together? This question seems to float in the cold winter air. The answer is naturally different for each couple, but they have one thing in common - the time to decide is here and now!

Many of your birth sign will be up for moving to a new place and they will make their plans reality in various parts of 2021.

Health. Your energy levels are quite high this month and there is no need to worry about your health.

CAPRICORN

A strange month lies ahead of you. It is time to tot up the score; one part of your life is ending and another beginning. You should run with your future as there seems to be no other option.

Business. After enduring many arguments and demands you will find some peace at last; your problems will soon be behind you and this becomes obvious to you in the second half of December. The question over disputed real estate, land or some other large property will reach a conclusion that suits both parties this time. In the future, your business can continue in its standard operating mode with your friends and those close to you helping you to resolve complex situations.

Clerical workers might change a job for a more interesting and better paid one. Some will have a real opportunity to do so in the second part of December, others in 2021.

Money. The financial situation will improve towards the end of the month and this positive trend is set to continue into 2021.

Love and family. You will finally sort out a complicated family situation this month. Couples going through a divorce will reach a settlement and thus be able to make plans for future.

Lovers enter a period when they have to consider many things and this difficult time will continue into 2021.

Looking further ahead, the stars recommend paying attention to your children as there might be problems related to them in the near future; the nature of the problem will only become clear in 2021, but there are grounds for concern.

Health. Your energy levels are not high this month, so try to stick to your limits and remember about the benefits of a good night's sleep.

AQUARIUS

You fall under the influence of two powerful planets - Jupiter and Saturn - in December. They open your eyes to both the past and to the future. Such co-incidences in the zodiac are very rare and if your fortune should indicate a path to you, follow it without reservation.

Business. A complicated period in your life is finished: this is equally true for those who have faced aggression from their partners from other cities or overseas; for those who have had a conflict with the authorities and their inspections or for those who have had prolonged legal issues. The battles are finally coming to their logical conclusion and you will now have a chance to get on with your business or to start something new; you need to be in good shape and totally prepared, however.

Opportunities that only begin to show themselves in the second part of December will fully unfurl next year. It is natural that these opportunities demand serious effort and responsibility of you. As your future depends on your decisions, you need to think everything through properly.

Money. December will be rather neutral financially; you cannot expect big earnings, but your expenses will be moderate and sensible.

Love and family. For those whose life is centered around love or family, the stars promise peace and tranquillity.

Your relationships with relatives who experienced grave situations in their lives eventually stabilize; there are reasons to believe that you will reconcile and that the protracted problems among your close relatives will cease. The situation is improving, but you will face other problems - this time connected to real estate - in the near future.

This will happen in 2021 and so you need to consider all the possible variants and take measures so as not to be caught flat footed.

Health. Even though your energy levels are quite high this month, you should be extra careful while driving and traveling between the 20th and the 25th of December.

PISCES

You are prepared to tackle all problems by yourself this time and December is the perfect time for action. Don't let up and you will succeed!

Business. December is one of the best months of the year for professional matters. You are making great strides and see that many issues you have been trying to resolve for some time are eventually being sorted out. Although you will gain a lot, it is not, of course, everything; it is only what you have earned. Thus, it seems as though a chapter of your career or even of your life has finished. You will have to re-organize and to search out the new paths and possibilities ahead. The end of December illustrates this, but you will only get a good idea about precisely how things will work out in 2021.

Clerical workers will have excellent opportunities to fully reveal their talents and you should not waste them. The forthcoming year, however, is complicated, and you will not receive any gratitude or acknowledgement of your efforts. Nevertheless, 2021 remains full of possibility for you!

Money. December is quite good financially. You will have regular inflows of cash and the amount will increase noticeably. The approximate dates for receiving large sums in December are the 5th, 6th, 13th, 14th, the 22nd to the 24th and the 31st.

Love and family. If December is pretty good from a professional point of view, the same cannot be said about your personal life. To be more exact, are you really proud of all the conflicts and arguments now in the past? Probably not but as you cannot change what you have done, you need to make a pause, reflect and draw the relevant conclusions for the whole year ahead. This is mainly true for those who spent much of 2020 fighting.

Strong couples will make a decision to change many things in their lives, in their usual routine and they will definitely realize their plans in 2021.

Health. Your energy levels are quite high this month and you should not worry about problems with health. You will celebrate the New Year among friends, children and those close to you. You will have a lot of fun!

Zodiac connections and us - a guide to compatibility

Often, when we meet a person, we get a feeling that they are good and we take an instant liking to them. Another person, however, gives us immediate feelings of distrust, fear and hostility. Is there an astrological reason why people say that 'the first impression is the most accurate'? How can we detect those who will bring us nothing but trouble and unhappiness?

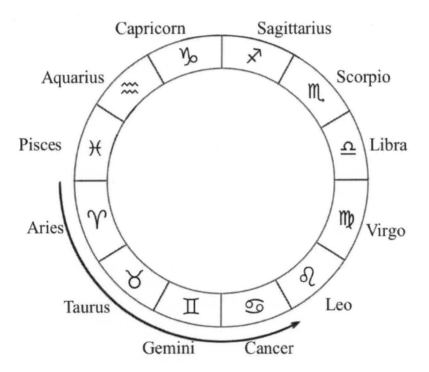

Without going too deeply into astrological subtleties unfamiliar to some readers, it is possible to determine the traits according to which friendship, love or business relationships will develop.

Let's begin with problematic relationships - our most difficult are with our 8th sign. For example, for Aries the 8th sign is Scorpio, for Taurus it is Sagittarius and so on. Finding your 8th sign is easy; assume your own sign to be first (see above Figure) and then move eight signs counter clockwise around the Zodiac circle. This is also how the other signs (fourth, ninth and so on) that we mention are to be found.

Ancient astrologers variously referred to the 8th sign as the symbol of death, of destruction, of fated love or unfathomable attraction. In astrological terms, this pair is called 'master and slave' or 'boa constrictor and rabbit', with the role of 'master' or 'boa constrictor' being played by our 8th sign.

This relationship is especially difficult for politicians and business people. We can take the example of a recent political confrontation in the USA. Hilary Clinton is a Scorpio while Donald Trump is a Gemini - her 8th sign. Even though many were certain that Clinton would be elected President, she lost.

To take another example, Hitler was a Taurus and his opponents – Stalin and Churchill - were both of his 8th sign, Sagittarius. The result of their confrontation is well known. Interestingly, the Russian Marshals who dealt crushing military blows to Hitler and so helped end the Third Reich - Konstantin Rokossovsky and Georgy Zhukov - were also Sagittarian, Hitler's 8th sign.

In another historical illustration, Lenin was also a Taurus. Stalin was of Lenin's 8th sign and was ultimately responsible for the downfall and possibly death of his one-time comrade-in-arms.

Business ties with those of our 8th sign are hazardous as they ultimately lead to stress and loss; both financial and moral. So, do not tangle with your 8th sign and never fight with it - your chances of winning are remote! Such relationships are very interesting in terms of love and romance, however. We are magnetically attracted to our 8th sign and even though it may be very intense physically, it is very difficult for family life; 'Feeling bad when together, feeling worse when apart'.

As an example, let us take the famous lovers - George Sand who was Cancer and Alfred de Musset who was Sagittarius. Cancer is the 8th sign for

Sagittarius, and the story of their crazy two-year love affair was the subject of much attention throughout France. Critics and writers were divided into 'Mussulist' and 'Sandist' camps; they debated fiercely about who was to blame for the sad ending to their love story - him or her. It's hard to imagine the energy needed to captivate the public for so long, but that energy was destructive for the couple. Passion raged in their hearts, but neither of them was able to comprehend their situation.

Georges Sand wrote to Musset, "I don't love you anymore, and I will always adore you. I don't want you anymore, and I can't do without you. It seems that nothing but a heavenly lightning strike can heal me by destroying me. Good-bye! Stay or go, but don't say that I am not suffering. This is the only thing that can make me suffer even more, my love, my life, my blood! Go away, but kill me, leaving." Musset replied only in brief, but its power surpassed Sand's tirade, "When you embraced me, I felt something that is still bothering me, making it impossible for me to approach another woman." These two people loved each other passionately and for two years lived together in a powder keg of passion, hatred and treachery.

When someone enters into a romantic liaison with their 8th sign, there will be no peace; indeed, these relationships are very attractive to those who enjoy the edgy, the borderline and, in the Dostoevsky style, the melodramatic. The first to lose interest in the relationship is, as a rule, the 8th sign.

If, by turn of fate, our child is born under our 8th sign, they will be very different from us and, in some ways, not live up to our expectations. It may be best to let them choose their own path.

In business and political relationships, the combination with our 12th sign is also a complicated one.

We can take two political examples. Angela Merkel is a Cancer while Donald Trump is a Gemini - her 12th sign. This is why their relations are strained and complicated and we can even perhaps assume that the American president will achieve his political goals at her expense. Boris Yeltsin (Aquarius) was the 12th sign to Mikhail Gorbachev (Pisces) and it was Yeltsin who managed to dethrone the champion of Perestroika.

Even ancient astrologers noticed that our relationships with our 12th signs can never develop evenly; it is one of the most curious and problematic combinations. They are our hidden enemies and they seem to be digging a hole for us; they ingratiate themselves with us, discover our innermost secrets. As a result, we become bewildered and make mistakes when we deal with them. Among the Roman emperors murdered by members of their entourage, there was an interesting pattern - all the murderers were the 12th sign of the murdered.

We can also see this pernicious effect in Russian history: the German princess Alexandra (Gemini) married the last Russian Tsar Nicholas II (Taurus) - he was her 12th sign and brought her a tragic death. The wicked genius Grigory Rasputin (Cancer) made friends with Tsarina Alexandra, who was his 12th sign, and was murdered as a result of their odd friendship. The weakness of Nicholas II was exposed, and his authority reduced after the death of the economic and social reformer Pyotr Stolypin, who was his 12th sign. Thus, we see a chain of people whose downfall was brought about by their 12th sign.

So, it makes sense to be cautious of your 12th sign, especially if you have business ties. Usually, these people know much more about us than we want them to and they will often reveal our secrets for personal gain if it suits them. However, the outset of these relationships is, as a rule, quite normal - sometimes the two people will be friends, but sooner or later one will betray the other one or divulge a secret; inadvertently or not.

In terms of romantic relationships, our 12th sign is gentle, they take care of us and are tender towards us. They know our weaknesses well but accept them with understanding. It is they who guide us, although sometimes almost imperceptibly. Sexual attraction is usually strong.
For example, Meghan Markle is a Leo, the 12th sign for Prince Harry, who is a Virgo. Despite Queen Elizabeth II being lukewarm about the match, Harry's love was so strong that they did marry.

If a child is our 12th sign, it later becomes clear that they know all our secrets, even those that they are not supposed to know. It is very difficult to control them as they do everything in their own way.
Relations with our 7th sign are also interesting. They are like our opposite; they have something to learn from us while we, in turn, have something to learn from them. This combination, in business and personal relationships, can be very positive and stimulating provided that both partners

193

are quite intelligent and have high moral standards but if not, constant misunderstandings and challenges follow. Marriage or co-operation with the 7th sign can only exist as the union of two fully-fledged individuals and in this case love, significant business achievements and social success are possible.

However, the combination can be not only interesting, but also quite complicated.

An example is Angelina Jolie, a Gemini, and Brad Pitt, a Sagittarius. This is a typical bond with a 7th sign - it's lively and interesting, but rather stressful. Although such a couple may quarrel and even part from time to time, never do they lose interest in each other.

This may be why this combination is more stable in middle-age when there is an understanding of the true nature of marriage and partnership. In global, political terms, this suggests a state of eternal tension - a cold war - for example between Yeltsin (Aquarius) and Bill Clinton (Leo).

Relations with our 9th sign are very good; they are our teacher and advisor - one who reveals things we are unaware of and our relationships with them very often involve travel or re-location. The combination can lead to spiritual growth and can be beneficial in terms of business.

Although, for example, Trump and Putin are political opponents, they can come to an understanding and even feel a certain sympathy for each other because Putin is a Libra while Trump is a Gemini, his 9th sign.

This union is also quite harmonious for conjugal and romantic relationships.

We treat our 3rd sign somewhat condescendingly. They are like our younger siblings; we teach them and expect them to listen attentively. Our younger brothers and sisters are more often than not born under this sign. In terms of personal and sexual relationships, the union is not very inspiring and can end quickly, although this is not always the case. In terms of business, it is fairly average as it often connects partners from different cities or countries.

We treat our 5th sign as a child and we must take care of them accordingly. The combination is not very good for business, however, since our 5th sign triumphs over us in terms of connections and finances, and thereby gives us very little in return save for love or sympathy. However, they are very good for family and romantic relationships, especially if the 5th sign is female. If a child is born as a 5th sign to their parents, their relationship will be a mutually smooth, loving and understanding one that lasts a lifetime.

Our 10th sign is a born leader. Depending on the spiritual level of those involved, both pleasant and tense relations are possible; the relationship is often mutually beneficial in the good times but mutually disruptive in the bad times. In family relations, our 10th sign always tries to lead and will do so according to their intelligence and upbringing.

Our 4th sign protects our home and can act as a sponsor to strengthen our financial or moral positions. Their advice should be heeded in all cases as it can be very effective, albeit very unobtrusive. If a woman takes this role, the relationship can be long and romantic, since all the spouse's wishes are usually met one way or another. Sometimes, such couples achieve great social success; for instance, Hilary Clinton, a Scorpio is the 4th sign to Bill Clinton, a Leo. On the other hand, if the husband is the 4th sign for his wife, he tends to be henpecked. There is often a strong sexual attraction. Our 4th sign can improve our living conditions and care for us in a parental way. If a child is our 4th sign, they are close to us and support us affectionately.

Relations with our 11th sign are often either friendly or patronizing; we treat them reverently, while they treat us with friendly condescension. Sometimes, these relationships develop in an 'older brother' or 'high-ranking friend' sense; indeed, older brothers and sisters are often our 11th sign. In terms of personal and sexual relationships, our 11th sign is always inclined to enslave us. This tendency is most clearly manifested in such alliances as Capricorn and Pisces or Leo and Libra. A child who is the 11th sign to their parents will achieve greater success than their parents, but this will only make the parents proud.

Our 2nd sign should bring us financial or other benefits; we receive a lot from them in both our business and our family life. In married couples, the 2nd sign usually looks after the financial situation for the benefit of the family. Sexual attraction is strong.

Our 6th sign is our 'slave'; we always benefit from working with them and it's very difficult for them to escape our influence. In the event of hostility, especially if they have provoked the conflict, they receive a powerful retaliatory strike. In personal relations, we can almost destroy them by making them dance to our tune. For example, if a husband doesn't allow his wife to work or there are other adverse family circumstances, she gradually becomes lost as an individual despite being surrounded by care. This is the best-case scenario; worse outcomes are possible. Our 6th sign has a strong sexual attraction to us because we are the fatal 8th sign for them; we cool down quickly, however, and often make all kinds of demands. If the relationship with our 6th sign is a long one, there is a danger that routine, boredom and stagnation will ultimately destroy the relationship. A child born under our 6th sign needs particularly careful handling as they can feel fear or embarrassment when communicating with us. Their health often needs increased attention and we should also remember that they are very different from us emotionally.

Finally, we turn to relations with our own sign. Scorpio with Scorpio and Cancer with Cancer get along well, but in most other cases, however, our own sign is of little interest to us as it has a similar energy. Sometimes, this relationship can develop as a rivalry, either in business or in love.

There is another interesting detail - we are often attracted to one particular sign. For example, a man's wife and mistress often have the same sign. If there is confrontation between the two, the stronger character displaces the weaker one. As an example, Prince Charles is a Scorpio, while both Princess Diana and Camilla Parker Bowles were born under the sign of Cancer. Camilla was the more assertive and became dominant.

Of course, in order to draw any definitive conclusions, we need an individually prepared horoscope, but the above always, one way or another, manifests itself.

Tatiana Borsch